REVEALING THE
MYSTERIES
OF HEAVEN

DR. DAVID JEREMIAH

with Dr. David Jeremiah

Edited by William Kruidenier
Unless otherwise indicated, Scripture verses quoted are taken from the NEW KING JAMES VERSION.

Printed in the United States of America.

CONTENTS

ABOUT
DR. DAVID JEREMIAH
AND TURNING POINT

D
r. David Jeremiah is the founder of Turning Point, a ministry committed to providing Christians with sound Bible teaching relevant to today's changing times through radio and television broadcasts, audio series, and books. Dr. Jeremiah's common-sense teaching on topics such as family, prayer, worship, angels, and biblical prophecy forms the foundation of Turning Point.

David and his wife, Donna, reside in El Cajon, California, where he serves as the senior pastor of Shadow Mountain Community Church. David and Donna have four children and eleven grandchildren.

In 1982, Dr. Jeremiah brought the same solid teaching to San Diego television that he shares weekly with his congregation. Shortly thereafter, Turning Point expanded its ministry to radio. Dr. Jeremiah's inspiring messages can now be heard worldwide on radio and television, and the Internet.

Because Dr. Jeremiah desires to know his listening audience, he travels nationwide holding ministry rallies and spiritual enrichment conferences that touch the hearts and lives of many people. According to Dr. Jeremiah, "At some point in time, everyone reaches a turning point; and for every person, that moment is unique, an experience to hold onto forever. There's so much changing in today's world that sometimes it's difficult to choose the right path. Turning Point offers people an understanding of God's Word as well as the opportunity to make a difference in their lives."

Dr. Jeremiah has authored numerous books, including *Escape the Coming Night* (Revelation), *The Handwriting on the Wall* (Daniel), *Overcoming Loneliness, Grand Parenting, The Joy of Encouragement, Prayer—The Great Adventure, God in You (Holy Spirit), Gifts from God (Parenting), Jesus' Final Warning, When Your World Falls Apart, Slaying the Giants in Your Life, My Heart's Desire, Sanctuary, Life Wide Open, Searching for Heaven on Earth, The Secret of the Light, Captured by Grace, Discover Paradise, Grace Givers, Why the Nativity?, Signs of Life, The 12 Ways of Christmas, 1 Minute a Day, What in the World Is Going On?* and *Living With Confidence in a Chaotic World.*

ABOUT THIS
STUDY GUIDE

The purpose of this Turning Point study guide is to reinforce Dr. David Jeremiah's dynamic, in-depth teaching and to aid the reader in applying biblical truth to his or her daily life. This study guide is designed to be used in conjunction with Dr. Jeremiah's *Revealing the Mysteries of Heaven* audio series, but it may also be used by itself for personal or group study.

STRUCTURE OF THE LESSONS

Each lesson is based on one of the messages in the *Revealing the Mysteries of Heaven* compact disc series and focuses on specific passages in the Bible. Each lesson is composed of the following elements:

- *Outline*

The outline at the beginning of the lesson gives a clear, concise picture of the topic being studied and provides a helpful framework for readers as they listen to Dr. Jeremiah's teaching.

- *Overview*

The overview summarizes Dr. Jeremiah's teaching on the passage being studied in the lesson. Readers should refer to the Scripture passages in their own Bibles as they study the overview.

- *Application*

This section contains a variety of questions designed to help readers dig deeper into the lesson and the Scriptures, and to apply the lesson to their daily lives. For Bible study groups or Sunday school classes, these questions will provide a springboard for group discussion and interaction.

- *Did You Know?*

This section presents a fascinating fact, historical note, or insight that adds a point of interest to the preceding lesson.

USING THIS GUIDE FOR GROUP STUDY

The lessons in this study guide are suitable for Sunday school classes, small-group studies, elective Bible studies, or home Bible study groups. Each person in the group should have his or her own study guide.

When possible, the study guide should be used with the corresponding compact disc series. You may wish to assign the study guide as homework prior to the meeting of the group and then use the meeting time to listen to the CD and discuss the lesson

FOR CONTINUING STUDY

For a complete listing of Dr. Jeremiah's materials for personal and group study call 1-800-947-1993, go online to www.DavidJeremiah.org, or write to: Turning Point, P.O. Box 3838, San Diego, CA 92163.

Dr. Jeremiah's *Turning Point* program is currently heard or viewed around the world on radio, television, and the Internet in English. *Momento Decisivo*, the Spanish translation of Dr. Jeremiah's messages, can be heard on radio in every Spanish speaking country in the world. The television broadcast is also broadcast by satellite throughout the Middle East with Arabic subtitles.

Contact Turning Point for radio and television program times and stations in your area. Or visit our website at www.DavidJeremiah.org.

REVEALING THE MYSTERIES OF HEAVEN

INTRODUCTION

Thomas Guthrie was a nineteenth century Scottish preacher and theologian who wrote, "If you find yourself loving any pleasure more than your prayers, any book better than the Bible, any house better than the house of the Lord, any table better than the Lord's table, any persons better than Christ, *or any indulgence better than the hope of heaven*—be alarmed." That last phrase is in italics (not in the original) because it highlights the focus of this study guide: *Revealing the Mysteries of Heaven.*

Intentionally or unintentionally, there are far too many Christians who find themselves loving the prospects of heaven less than they do many of the indulgences of this world. And in the words of the Scottish divine, we should be alarmed at that reality. The writer of the letter to the Hebrews had it right: there are many weights and sins that so easily ensnare us in this world, causing us to take our eyes off Jesus, "the author and finisher of our faith." We fail to see him sitting "at the right hand of the throne of God" in heaven—the very heaven that is the destination of those who believe in Him (Hebrews 12:1-2).

"Out of sight, out of mind" is a proven truism—and heaven is definitely out of our human sight. The only way to keep heaven in our mind's eye is to read and rehearse the truths about heaven found in the Word of God. But even when we do that, we find there are many things about heaven that are not easy to understand. After all, it is not like earth, we have never visited it, and we have no photographs to whet our appetite and our longing to be there. We are left with Scripture alone to inform us about our eternal home and answer the many questions that arise.

For instance, how real a place is heaven? Is it an actual physical place just like earth, or is it a wispy, ethereal domain suited for spiritual, not physical, beings? And why does Paul mention a third heaven—which implies a first and second? Why are there three heavens?

If there is a heaven, does that mean there is also a hell? And what is purgatory? Is that a real place—an intermediate location on the way to heaven or hell?

It sounds sacrilegious, but won't heaven be boring? There is a popular image in our culture of sitting on clouds playing harps all day. Or taking a stroll down streets paved with gold, going in and out the pearly gates. And all this for eternity! Why should I expect heaven not to be boring?

What changes will human beings undergo before they enter heaven? Will they inhabit bodies as they do on earth? If so, what kind of bodies?

What is the connection between how I live on earth and what heaven will be like? I know I'm not saved by my works, but surely how faithfully I live as a Christian has some bearing on my eternal existence. The New Testament talks about rewards—what are the rewards and how are they given?

Where exactly are we going to live in heaven? Jesus said He was going to prepare a place for us, so what is that place?

These questions and more—like, What happens to planet earth? Is the Millennium part of heaven? Do children go to heaven?—will be answered in *Revealing the Mysteries of Heaven*. The goal is to provide answers to the questions Christians have in order to make our eternal home as real "on earth as it is in heaven."

WHAT'S UP WITH HEAVEN?

Selected Scriptures

*In this lesson we learn why heaven is
such an important place for the Christian.*

OUTLINE

Everyone has heard the expression, "Oh, this is just heaven!"
Granted, it's a figure of speech, but it betrays the casual approach
most people take to something that is biblically serious. Since
heaven is the eternal home of Christians, we should know all there
is to know about it.

I. The Prominence of Heaven

II. The Plurality of Heaven
 A. The First Heaven
 B. The Second Heaven
 C. The Third Heaven

III. The Place Called Heaven

IV. The Preciousness of Heaven
 A. Our Redeemer Is in Heaven
 B. Our Relationships Are in Heaven
 C. Our Resources Are in Heaven
 D. Our Residence Is in Heaven
 E. Our Reward Is in Heaven
 F. Our Riches Are in Heaven
 G. Our Reservation Is in Heaven

W hen a Sunday school teacher quizzed her class of fifth-graders about how one gets to heaven, she got all correct answers: One doesn't get there by being good, giving away money, or being a nice person. "Well, then," she asked, "how *does* one get to heaven?" Before any of the regular students could answer, a boy who was visiting the class that week shouted out, "You have to be dead!"

That's the correct answer, isn't it? Unless Jesus Christ returns and takes us off the earth to be with Him in heaven, we have to die to get there. Worldwide, three people die every second. That means nearly 11,000 people every hour are passing from life to death and going either to heaven or to hell—nearly 260,000 people every day.[1]

A 2003 Harris Poll found that 82 percent of Americans believe in heaven and 63 percent said they expected to go there when they die. In spite of all that interest in heaven, there is little talk about heaven in American churches whether evangelical, mainline Protestant, or Catholic.[2]

Other polls from the Barna and Gallup organizations tell us there is little difference between the morals and lifestyles of Christians and non-Christians. And I believe the absence of a focus on heaven is in large part to blame. When we lose sight of the fact that God has a wonderful destination prepared for those who are His, we start trying to create heaven on earth. We start investing our time and talent and treasure in creating a place that we know in our heart is what we were created for (Ecclesiastes 3:11). We know there is supposed to be a heaven; and when we stop seeking the biblical heaven, we try to create an earthly one.

The problem with that strategy is that we could never approximate on earth what God has created for us in heaven—so we try harder. And we begin pursuing the pleasures of this world. We begin doing what Solomon writes about in Ecclesiastes, looking for pleasure and satisfaction in wine, women, and wealth. He finally recognized the futility (vanity) of his ways, but many Christians have not. If we do not feed the hunger for heaven with biblical truth, we will feed it the superficial baubles and bangles of this world.

THE PROMINENCE OF HEAVEN

While heaven isn't being talked about much in churches, it seems to be popping up in the popular culture. A book called *The Five People You Meet in Heaven*, by Mitch Albom, was on the

New York Time's bestseller list for more than a year—but it has nothing to do with heaven. It has to do with evaluating how you treated people on earth when you meet them in heaven. The famous *Left Behind* series has sold millions of books and deals a lot with heaven. And a book called *Heaven* by an evangelical author, Randy Alcorn, was recently published and sold a hundred thousand copies in just a few months. So people are reading about heaven—we're just not talking about it in church very much.

Heaven is mentioned over 500 times in Scripture. Both the Old Testament (*shamayim*) and the New Testament (*ouranos*) words for heaven refer to high and lofty places. Heaven is a consistent theme in the Bible. It is discussed in our culture, but the average Christian knows little about it.

THE PLURALITY OF HEAVEN

The Bible speaks of three heavens. Paul, when writing to the Corinthian believers, talks about being "caught up to the third heaven" (2 Corinthians 12:2), a place he then refers to as "Paradise" (verse 4). We have to conclude that if Paul visited the third heaven, there must be a first and second heaven as well.

The First Heaven (Isaiah 55:9–10)

We could call this heaven the "atmospheric" heaven—a place mentioned numerous times in Scripture: "For as the heavens are higher than the earth . . . . For as the rain comes down . . . from heaven" (Isaiah 55:9–10). This heaven is the atmosphere surrounding the earth—the domain of clouds and birds (Genesis 1:20).

The Second Heaven (Genesis 1:14–17)

This heaven is mentioned early in the book of Genesis and is the domain of the heavenly bodies: the sun, moon, stars, planets, and galaxies besides our own. We refer to this today as "outer space" where satellites and planetary space probes travel.

The Third Heaven (2 Corinthians 12:2–4)

When Paul described being caught up to the third heaven, he didn't say where it was. In fact, he seemed not to know: ". . . whether in the body I do not know, or whether out of the body I do not know." We can only assume it was a place beyond the atmospheric and stellar heavens—the dwelling place of God.

Jesus taught His disciples to pray, "Our Father in heaven . . ." (Matthew 6:9), and referred in Matthew 5:16 to "your Father in heaven." Psalm 11:4 says, "The Lord's throne is in heaven." That must be the heaven to which Paul was taken by God—either physically or spiritually—the heaven where God dwells. This is the heaven that is our destination as believers in Christ.

The Place Called Heaven

John 14 is a classic text on the subject of heaven where we learn from Jesus Christ himself as He raised the subject with His disciples.

The disciples of Christ were greatly troubled at the timeline that had been laid out for them concerning Jesus' future: He would die, be buried, be resurrected, and then return to heaven. Not understanding the complete picture of Christ's mission, they were understandably sorrowful at this news that He was going to leave them. But in John 14:1–4, He gives them a truth to comfort them in their sorrows: "I'm going to prepare a place for you in my Father's house so that you can one day join Me there forever" (paraphrase).

Then Jesus replied to Thomas's doubts (verse 5) by saying, "No one comes to the Father except through Me" (verse 6b). That is, not just His disciples would be joining Him in heaven, but all who believed in Him. Heaven is a real place being prepared by Christ to receive all those who belong to Him. Jesus didn't leave His disciples or us to find heaven on earth. He went to prepare heaven for us.

While heaven is referred to in Jesus' parables by many metaphors (country, city, kingdom), the picture I like best is the one here in John 14: the Father's house. Those who grew up in a warm and loving house know it as a place you long to return to. When we were younger, my wife and I would drive two thousand miles round trip over a weekend just to spend a few hours in "the father's house." When my dad eventually became a widower and sold the home place, I hated to see us lose it because of what it represented: The place to which we could always return.

Fortunately, we don't have to worry about losing our heavenly Father's house since Christ has gone to heaven to prepare it for us. It is a permanent heavenly abode where we will dwell forever in God's presence. Heaven is not a feeling or an emotion or a point of view or an attitude. It is not a place we create by our actions here on earth. It is a "place" (Greek *topos*, in John 14:2; a physical, locatable place).

Where, exactly, is the place called heaven? We can't say with certainty because the Bible doesn't say. But Ephesians 4:10 says it is above all the heavens, where Christ ascended; and in Acts 1:10–11, the disciples were gazing "up into heaven" where Jesus had gone.

If language means anything, we have to assume that Jesus' destination was "up."

But depending upon where you are standing on earth, "up" is a different direction—it just means perpendicular to the surface of the planet. But in Isaiah 14, we get a different perspective. Addressing God, Satan says, "I will exalt my throne above the stars of God; I will also sit on the mount of the congregation on the farthest sides of the north" (verse 13). Satan refers to heaven as the "farthest sides of the north." Regardless of where you are on the globe, north is always pointing in the same direction. So it may be reasonable to conclude that heaven is somewhere in the northern heavens beyond the range of the astronomers' most powerful telescopes. Astronomers even tell us that this part of outer space contains fewer stars and galaxies than other parts.

So, even if we don't know exactly where the third heaven is, we know it's a specific place where Jesus is preparing a place for us.

THE PRECIOUSNESS OF HEAVEN

Everything that should be precious to a follower of Christ applies to heaven because that's where Christ is, where He will be forever, and where we will be with Him. Here are seven reasons why heaven is a precious place.

Our Redeemer Is in Heaven

Hebrews 9:24 says Christ has entered "into heaven itself, now to appear in the presence of God for us." The descriptions of heaven in Revelation suggest it is going to be a stunningly beautiful place, but I believe all that beauty will pale into insignificance when we behold the beauty of our Redeemer, Jesus Christ. When we see the One who suffered and died to pay the penalty for our sins . . . when we see the scars of His suffering, I think nothing will look as beautiful as He will look to our eyes when we see Him as He really is.

Our Relationships Are in Heaven

My father told me as he grew old and began to see his friends pass away, "One of the hard things about getting old is you have more friends in heaven than you do on earth." That's true, but what a wonderful truth! My wife and I have lost all four of our parents, but we know where they are—they are in heaven. And we rejoice that one day we will be reunited with them.

The writer to the Hebrews made an interesting choice of words when he wrote, "To the general assembly and church of the firstborn who are registered in heaven" (12:23). It sounds like checking in at a hotel, doesn't it? You leave earth and arrive in heaven and are registered there. So when we get there, we will look up our friends and loved ones and be reunited for all eternity.

Our Resources Are in Heaven

First Peter 1:3–4 says that our inheritance is "reserved in heaven." When you became a Christian, God became your Father. And when God is your Father, you are one of His heirs, which means you have an inheritance waiting for you in heaven. Peter says that inheritance has preceded us to heaven—it is already there waiting for us to arrive and claim it. Unlike earthly inheritances, our heavenly inheritance is not dependent on the economy as to its value. It has been perfectly established in heaven and will never change.

Our Residence Is in Heaven

Philippians 3:20 says that "our citizenship is in heaven." That doesn't mean we reside there now, but it does mean that's our official, permanent residence. When we fill out paperwork in this life, we have to declare our place of birth and our residence— but that's all just temporary. Our real place of birth is heaven (the phrase in Greek, "born again," can also be translated "born from above" John 3:3, 7); and therefore our citizenship is in heaven. When we die, we simply go to our permanent home to live for eternity.

Our Reward Is in Heaven

Jesus told His disciples to "rejoice and be exceedingly glad, for great is your reward in heaven" (Matthew 5:12). We will spend an entire lesson in this series on the rewards of heaven. As a preview, we can note here that there are five crowns that can be earned by Christians on earth, crowns which will be awarded in heaven.

Some think it is not very spiritual to be looking forward to heaven in order to receive a reward. But God is big on rewards! All throughout Scripture, God makes promises that have positive benefits as their rewards. God motivates us to faithfulness by offering rewards. That is perfectly reasonable since our fallen human nature is not inclined to be faithful or obedient. So God motivates us to be faithful and then rewards us when we are. It's a great program!

Amazingly, we will end up casting all those crowns and rewards at the feet of Jesus in honor and praise of Him (Revelation 4:10; more on this in an upcoming lesson).

Our Riches Are in Heaven

Another reason why heaven is so precious is that our riches are in heaven. In Matthew 6:19–21, Jesus tells His followers not to lay up treasures on earth, but to lay them up in heaven where they would be eternally safe: "For where your treasure is, there your heart will be also" (verse 21).

How do we store up treasure in heaven? By investing on earth in the only things that are going to be transferred to heaven, and that is the souls of men and women and boys and girls. The Word of God and the human soul are the only eternal things on earth. So to build equity in heaven, we have to build the Word of God into the lives of people on earth.

Our Reservation Is in Heaven

Revelation 21:27 says that "only those who are written in the Lamb's Book of Life" will be allowed into heaven. If you belong to Christ, then your name is recorded in that book in heaven. Jesus once told His disciples to rejoice that their names were "written in heaven" (Luke 10:20)—and we should likewise rejoice.

As we begin this series of eleven lessons on the subject of heaven, it's the right time for you to confirm that your name is written in the Lamb's Book of Life. If you have never asked God to forgive your sins through Christ's death in your place on the cross, do so now. Heaven is not a place you want to miss!

Notes:

1. Randy Alcorn, *Heaven* (Wheaton: Tyndale House Publishers, 2004), xxi.

2. Cary McMullen, "Heaven: A Lot of Questions, But No One Really Knows the Answers," *The Ledger*, 27 March 2005.

1. What does the plural "heavens" in Genesis 1:1 suggest about how many heavens there are? *In the beginning, God created the heavens and the earth.*

   a. Which heaven did the apostle Paul visit? (2 Corinthians 12:2)
   Paul was caught up to the third heaven.

   b. If there is a "third" heaven, at least how many divisions of heaven must there be? *There are three heavens.*
   1st heaven is the atmospheric heaven.
   2nd heaven is outer space, stellar heaven.
   3rd The dwelling place of God.

   c. What characterizes the layer of heaven that is nearest to earth? (Genesis 7:11; 8:12; Psalm 78:23; Daniel 7:13)
   The 2nd heaven, the domain of the heavenly bodies, galaxies besides our own.

   d. What characterizes the next highest level of heaven? (Genesis 1:14-19; Psalm 19:4-6).

   e. What other word did Paul use to describe the "third heaven?" (2 Corinthians 12:4)

   f. What do you learn about this part of heaven from Luke 23:43 and Revelation 2:7?

   g. Though 2 Corinthians 5:8 doesn't use the word "heaven," how is it consistent with Luke 23:43?

2. What details about heaven can you discover from John 14:1-4?

  a. What Jesus called it: (verse 2)

  b. Why Jesus was going there: (verse 2)

  c. Who the future occupants will be: (verse 3)

  d. What level of comfort the anticipation of heaven should provide: (verse 1)

3. In what way did the apostle Paul "visit" the third heaven? (2 Corinthians 12:1-2)

  a. What kinds of things do you think Paul learned in his "trip"? (verse 4)

b. Why do you think Paul was chosen for these revelations in spite of being "the least of the apostles"? (1 Corinthians 15:9)

c. Given the repetition of the word "revelation" in 2 Corinthians 12:1 and Ephesians 3:3, what might Paul have been shown while in the third heaven? (Ephesians 3:2-6).

4. What clues in 1 Kings 8:27 and Nehemiah 9:6 suggest that the "third heaven" might be the ultimate level of heaven? (Clue: compare phrases like "Song of Songs" and "King of Kings." Who dwells in the "heaven of heavens"? (Nehemiah 9:6; Matthew 24:36)

DID YOU KNOW?

An obscure reference to the "queen of heaven" occurs five times in the Book of Jeremiah (7:18; 44:17, 18, 19, 25). The "queen" is not named but was undoubtedly a female goddess in the pagan pantheon of the day (possibly Ishtar, a female Babylonian deity). Jeremiah 7:18 mentions the involvement of the whole family in worshiping the "queen of heaven": "The children gather wood, the fathers kindle the fire, and the women knead dough, to make cakes for the queen of heaven." In addition to making cakes, the Israelites burned incense and poured out drink offerings to this pagan deity (44:18, 19). Heaven and its occupants were a focus of speculation among ancient peoples—and even Israelites who had rejected the God of heaven.

WHERE ARE THEY NOW?

Luke 16:19–31

*In this lesson we read a story that illustrates
the two eternal destinations of mankind.*

OUTLINE

It is common for armchair theologians to voice strong opinions concerning heaven and hell. Rather than speculate on such matters, it is far better to take the word of the Son of God himself from the story He told of two men—one who went to each place.

I. Two People
   A. Two Men Contrasted in Life
   B. Two Men Contrasted in Death
   C. Two Men Contrasted in Eternity

II. Two Places
   A. An Intermediate Hell: Hades
   B. An Intermediate Heaven: Paradise

III. Two Principles
   A. The Priority of the Presence of Jesus
   B. The Permanence of Personal Decisions

An Indiana cemetery has a tombstone more than one hundred years old with the following epitaph on it:

"Pause, stranger, when you pass me by:
As you are now, so once was I.
As I am now, so you will be.
Prepare for death and follow me."

Some wise person came along and added this thought beneath the poem:

"To follow you, I'm not content,
Until I know which way you went." [1]

There is an organization called Afterlife Telegrams that, for a charge, will deliver your message to a deceased person. They do this by hiring a terminally ill patient to promise to deliver the message when they get to "the other side." However, in the fine print on their agreement, they say delivery isn't guaranteed because no one actually knows what happens when someone dies.[2]

Everyone wants to know what happens to people when they die: Where and how are they? But that's not just a modern cause for concern. Paul wrote to the Thessalonian Christians so they would not be ignorant "concerning those who have fallen asleep" (1 Thessalonians 4:13). Falling asleep was, of course, a metaphor for death—the same one Jesus used to describe Lazarus (John 11:11). Dr. Luke described Stephen's death as falling asleep (Acts 7:60), and Paul described the death of David in the Old Testament the same way (Acts 13:36).

When people ask, "Where is my loved one now?" following his or her death, they obviously are not asking about the body. They're asking about the person's soul—their true being. The material body is laid in the grave, but what happens to the immaterial person? The Bible has the answer, and it is illustrated clearly in a story told by Jesus about two individuals who went to two different places when they died.

Two People (Luke 16:19–31)

In Luke 16 we have Jesus' story of two men: A rich man and a poor man named Lazarus.

Two Men Contrasted in Life (Luke 16:19–21)

- The rich man was covered in purple and fine linen, and the poor man, Lazarus, was covered with sores.
- The rich man fared sumptuously, while Lazarus subsisted only on crumbs.
- The rich man had many servants, while Lazarus had only the dogs to care for him.

Two Men Contrasted in Death (Luke 16:22)

From the story we gather that Lazarus died first. As a poor man, his body was perhaps buried either in the potter's field (Matthew 27:7) or thrown into Gehenna, the dump outside the city of Jerusalem. But Lazarus' soul, his real person, was "carried by the angels to Abraham's bosom." Then the rich man "died and was buried," probably with a lavish funeral.

So two men died—one disposed of as human debris while the other was buried with a grand funeral. They were different in life, different in death—and now we see the most important difference of all, their difference in eternity.

Two Men Contrasted in Eternity (16:22)

Before the ascension of Christ into heaven, following His resurrection from the dead, there was a place where the souls of the departed went at death. There were three divisions, or compartments, in that place: Abraham's bosom, the great gulf fixed, and hades, the place of torment.

Abraham's bosom was also called paradise, the abode of the righteous dead. This was the destination of Lazarus following his death. It was a place of comfort, love, and companionship.

The place of torment was also called hades, and it was the abode of the unrighteous dead (Luke 16:23). This is where the rich man went in Jesus' story.

In between these two places was a "great gulf" (Luke 16:26) that could not be crossed.

1. Lazarus in Eternity (Luke 16:22a)

    When I first began doing funerals as a young pastor, there would be older saints at the funeral who would say, "The angels just took her on to heaven." I wasn't sure where they got that perspective until I learned that's what happened to Lazarus: The angels carried him to Abraham's bosom. Again, this is another term for paradise, the place where the souls and spirits of Old Testament saints went when they died. Remember, this is an "Old Testament" story because it precedes the death, resurrection, and ascension of Christ.

So, Lazarus died and went to paradise, the place of comfort.

2. The Rich Man in Eternity (Luke 16:23–31)

The rich man did not fare so well. The place to which he went was a place of misery.

a. He Is in a Place of Misery (Luke 16:23–24)

Here is one of the clearest pictures in the Bible that the abode of the unrighteous dead is a place of flames (verse 24). The rich man begs "Father Abraham" to send Lazarus to give him a drink, ". . . for I am tormented in this flame." Lazarus and the rich man have exchanged places in death. The rich man in life has become the beggar in eternity, and vice versa.

b. He Is in a Place of Memory (Luke 16:25)

Verse 25 confirms that memory is not lost in eternity. Abraham reminded the rich man of what he had before he died, and how Lazarus is now the one who is comforted. I believe that throughout eternity the unbeliever will be reminded of what he missed due to rejecting the gospel of Christ. He will remember forever the opportunity he had, but which he rejected, to receive Christ and go to heaven instead of hell.

c. He Is in a Place of Mourning (Luke 16:27–31)

Misery and memory result in hades being a place of mourning. The rich man begs Abraham to send Lazarus to the rich man's family to warn them of the path they are on so they will not end up where he is. But Abraham says if they won't listen to Moses and the prophets, they won't listen to someone who returns from the dead. What this means is that the preaching of the Word of God is more powerful than if someone returns from the dead to warn of the torment that is to come.

TWO PLACES

We've talked about the two people involved, and we'll look now at the two places where they went.

An Intermediate Hell: Hades

Hades is not the ultimate, eternal hell where unbelievers will reside, but is an intermediate hell until the time of the Great White Throne Judgment (Revelation 20:11–14). Revelation says that, "Death and Hades delivered up the dead who were in them. And they were judged . . . ."

When a person dies today without knowing Christ, that person's body goes in the grave and his soul and spirit go to hades. After the judgment at the Great White Throne, death and hades give up those who were in them, and they are all cast into the lake of fire forever.

People ask me if I believe hell is forever, and I say "Yes—if there is no eternal hell, then there is no eternal heaven." The Bible says more about hell than it does about heaven, and our opinions on the subject make no difference at all. Hell is what the Bible says it is.

An Intermediate Heaven: Paradise

Just as there is an intermediate hell, so there is an intermediate heaven. Every believer who died before Christ ascended to heaven went to paradise. But when Jesus ascended to the Father (Acts 1:9), things changed in the eternal destiny of the righteous dead. Ephesians 4:8–10 says,

"Therefore He says:

'When He ascended on high,
He led captivity captive,
And gave gifts to men.'

"(Now this, 'He ascended'—what does it mean but that He also first descended into the lower parts of the earth? He who descended is also the One who ascended far above all the heavens, that He might fill all things.)"

When Jesus ascended to heaven after His resurrection, He went to paradise and gathered those believers who were there and took them with Him to paradise, the third heaven (2 Corinthians 12:2–4), into the presence of God. When Jesus was on the cross, He told the thief who believed in Him, "Assuredly, I say to you, today you will be with Me in Paradise" (Luke 23:43). And Paul equates paradise with the third heaven in 2 Corinthians 12:2–4. Therefore, paradise today is in the third heaven where Jesus Christ is, in the presence of God.

So, we have established that when believers die, their bodies go into the grave where they await the resurrection of the body at the Rapture, when they are raised to meet Christ in the air (1 Thessalonians 4:16–17). But what form do they take in the interim? Their bodies are in the grave and their spirits and souls are in paradise with Christ. But what exactly is our state while we are in paradise?

We have an indication in 2 Corinthians 5:1–5. Paul says the human spirit does not want to be unclothed, that is, separated from its body. And he says that when our earthly tent is torn down (we die), "we have a building from God, a house not made with hands, eternal in the heavens." So we get an intermediate body of some kind while we are in heaven, awaiting the resurrection of our original, physical bodies. We are not told exactly what it will look like—all I can imagine is that it is the manifestation of the spirit, the real person, in bodily form.

So, to review, when an Old Testament unbeliever died, his body went into the grave, and the soul and spirit goes to hades, where it remains until the Great White Throne Judgment when hades is thrown into the lake of fire forever. When an Old Testament believer died, his body went into the grave and his soul and spirit went to paradise. When Christ ascended to heaven, He took the occupants of paradise to the third heaven into the presence of God where they remain in an intermediate body until being reunited with their physical bodies at the Rapture. Since Christ's ascension into heaven, believers go to the third heaven also to await the Rapture and the resurrection of their physical bodies. Following the Rapture, all believers will always be "with the Lord" (1 Thessalonians 4:17).

Two Principles

To go with the two people and two places we've discussed, there are two principles that help to simplify what can seem like a complex scenario.

The Priority of the Presence of Jesus

We can get specific and detailed about the technicalities of heaven, but it boils down to this: Heaven is where Jesus is. The most important thing about heaven is that it's where Jesus Christ is and where He has promised to take us (John 14:1–4). When Jesus spoke to the thief on the cross He said, "Today you will be with Me . . ." (Luke 23:43). Paul said that to be absent from the body is to be present with the Lord (2 Corinthians 5:8). When Paul wrote to the Philippians, he didn't say he was hard-pressed between wanting to be with the Philippians or going to heaven. He said he was hard-pressed between being with the Philippians and being with Christ (Philippians 1:23–24). The priority is not being in heaven, it's being with Christ. Wherever heaven is, as long as Christ is there, we'll be fine. It wasn't heaven that saved us, it was Jesus. It wasn't heaven that is coming again for us, it's Jesus. So the priority is being with Him.

The best summary statement of all is Paul's when he wrote to the Thessalonians: "And thus we shall always be with the Lord" (1 Thessalonians 4:17). It's fine to know the what, why, when, where, and how—but most important is to know the "who," Jesus himself.

Richard Baxter said it this way:

"My knowledge of that life is small,
The eye of faith is dim;
But it's enough that Christ knows all,
And I shall be with Him." [3]

The Permanence of Personal Decisions (Luke 16:26)

In Jesus' story of Lazarus and the rich man, Abraham described a "great gulf fixed" between hades and paradise, "so that those who want to pass from here to you cannot, nor can those from there pass to us" (Luke 16:26). The gulf is fixed and is therefore permanent between heaven and hell.

The decision we make about eternity will be made in this life, and there will be no crossing from one side to the other after death. There is no such place as purgatory where we can earn our way into heaven. The Bible says, "And as it is appointed for men to die once, but after this the judgment" (Hebrews 9:27). The only thing that follows death is judgment. There is no state in which transactions are made allowing one to change his eternal destination. Whatever decisions are made about eternity will be made in this life. Paul wrote, "Behold, now is the day of salvation" (2 Corinthians 6:2).

I had gone to Alabama to speak at a prayer breakfast, and a man was waiting to talk with me when I arrived. He called himself "Red," and looked to be a man who'd had a hard life. But he enthusiastically told me his story.

Red had been down on his fortune and had decided to end his life by driving his car at a high rate of speed into a large tree that was on the edge of a local road. When he got in his car, he tried to find his favorite rock-and-roll station to turn the music up as loud as possible, but his radio was acting up. When he started hitting the radio with his hand, suddenly the Turning Point radio program came on; and he heard me talking about God's love, accepting Christ, and going to heaven. To make a long story short, he received Christ right there in his car and was born again—and began his journey to heaven. His life was changed dramatically, and he's now serving with a ministry that reaches out to hurting people.

The prospect of spending eternity with Christ in heaven is powerful, but it requires a decision on your part. I hope you have made the same decision Red did—that your eternity is secure with Christ in heaven.

Notes:

1. Ron Rhodes, *The Undiscovered Country: Exploring the Wonder of Heaven and the Afterlife* (Eugene: Harvest House, 1960), 39–40.

2. www.afterlifetelegrams.com /AFTERLIFE/Afterlife_Tele.htm.

3. Quoted by J. I. Packer in "Hell's Final Enigma," *Christianity Today*, April 4, 2002.

1. The Hebrew word *she'ol* denotes the place of the afterlife in the Old Testament and should be translated as "the grave" or as Sheol, rather than hell. What do you learn about Sheol in the following verses?

   a. It was a place of_____. (2 Samuel 22:6; Psalm 18:5)

   b. Sheol was below ground but still visible to_____. (Job 26:6)

   c. The psalmist anticipated that he would be_____ from Sheol. (Psalm 16:10)

   d. How is Sheol pictured with human traits in Proverbs 1:12 and Isaiah 5:14?

   e. What "underground" references are found in Isaiah 14:11?

2. Even though the immediate destination of the dead was "the grave," what ultimate hope did the psalmist express in Psalm 73:23-25?

    a. What does the word "heaven" suggest about his understanding of God's location?

    b. What does "glory" represent in the psalmist's mind? In spite of his troubles (verse 24), what does he think the future holds?

3. Read Daniel 12:1-3.

    a. At the end of the age, what will happen to those who have been in the grave? (verse 2)

    b. Some will awake to_____ _____ and some

    to_____ and_____ _____.

    (verse 2b)

c. What words in verse 3 parallel the suggestion of "glory" in Psalm 73:14?

d. How do the two categories of people in verse 2 parallel the two categories in Psalm 1:6?

e. At the final judgment, what will happen to "the ungodly"? (Psalm 1:5)

4. Read Job 19:25-27.

a. To what does destroyed skin refer in verse 26(a)?

b. What did Job anticipate even after his body had deteriorated in the grave? (verse 26b)

c. How does 1 Corinthians 15:51-53 confirm Job's anticipation?

5. What level of confidence do you have about your eternal destiny?

The most consistent Greek word translated "hell" in the New Testament is *geenna,* rendered Gehennah in English. Greek *geenna* derives from Hebrew *ge ben Hinnom*—valley of the son of Hinnom, mentioned 10 times in the Old Testament (for example, Joshua 15:8). It was a valley south and southwest of Jerusalem where Israelites participated in pagan idol worship and child sacrifice (Jeremiah 32:30-35). Jeremiah prophesied it would become a place of God's judgment (Jeremiah 7:30-32; 19:2, 6). By the first century A.D. it had become a smoldering trash heap where refuse, even dead bodies of criminals, were thrown to burn. Jesus used it frequently as an appropriate image of God's final judgment—"hell . . . the fire that shall never be quenched" (Mark 9:43).

Won't Heaven Be Boring?

Selected Scriptures

In this lesson we learn why heaven will never be boring!

OUTLINE

Some people suggest that heaven is going to be dull, sitting around strumming on harps all day—forever! Nothing could be farther from the truth. Heaven is the place where every ultimate longing of the human heart and spirit is satisfied, something we've never experienced on earth.

I. **Heaven Will Not Be Boring Because God Is Not Boring**

II. **Heaven Will Not Be Boring Because You Will Not Be Boring**

III. **Heaven Will Not Be Boring Because Your Friends Will Not Be Boring**

IV. **Heaven Will Not Be Boring Because Your Work Will Not Be Boring**

V. **Heaven Will Not Be Boring Because Heaven Is the Place You've Always Longed For**

Here's another epitaph for your collection that goes along with this lesson:

"Here lies a poor woman who always was tired,
For she lived in a place where help wasn't hired.
Her last words on earth were, 'Dear Friends, I am going,
Where washing ain't done, nor sweeping, nor sewing;
And everything there is exact to my wishes,
For where they don't eat, there's no washing of dishes.
Don't weep for me now, don't weep for me ever;
I'm going to do nothing for ever and ever.'" [1]

That's how a lot of people think about heaven—that it's going to be a place where we do nothing. In other words, a place that's b-o-o-o-r-i-n-g! But that is not true, and we'll see why in this lesson.

In his profound book, *Man in Search of Meaning,* Viktor Frankl wrote that:

"In actual fact, boredom is now causing, and . . . bringing psychiatrists . . . more problems to solve than distress. And these problems are growing increasingly crucial." [2]

It's as if we are still children: "Mommy, I'm bored!" As bored as people are now when they have things to do, they think they're going to be eternally bored in heaven where there is nothing to do.

Science fiction writer Isaac Asimov writes, "I don't believe in the afterlife, so I don't have to spend my whole life fearing hell or fearing heaven even more. For whatever the tortures of hell, I think the boredom of heaven would be even worse." [3]

In his book, *The Journey of Desire,* John Eldredge, writes, "Nearly every Christian I have spoken with has some idea that eternity is an unending church service . . . . We have settled on the image of the never-ending sing-along in the sky, one great hymn after another, forever and ever, amen. And our heart sinks, 'Forever and ever? That's it? That's the good news?' And then we sigh and [we] feel guilty. We feel guilty that we are not more 'spiritual.' We lose heart and we turn once more to the present to find [all the] life we can." [4]

In this lesson, I want to give you five reasons why heaven will not be boring—and I believe they will be reasons you may not have considered before.

Heaven Will Not Be
Boring Because God Is
Not Boring (Psalm 16:11)

Psalm 16:11 is a verse full of subtle implications about the excitement of being in God's presence: "You will show me the path of life; in Your presence is fullness of joy; at Your right hand are pleasures forevermore." I can't imagine anyone thinking that dwelling at the right hand of God (the position of His favor) would be boring! Where did this idea come from that God and His heaven are boring?

Randy Alcorn, who has written the definitive book on heaven says, "Our belief that heaven will be boring betrays a heresy—that God is boring. There is no greater nonsense. Our desire for pleasure and the experience of joy come directly from God's hands. He made our taste buds, adrenaline, sex (desires), and the nerve endings that convey pleasure to our brains. Likewise, our imaginations and our capacity for joy and exhilaration were made by the very God we accuse of being boring. Are we so arrogant that we imagine that human beings came up with the idea of having fun?

"The very qualities that you and I admire in others—every one of them—are true of God. He's the source of everything that you and I find fascinating. Who made Bach, [who made] Beethoven, [who made] Mozart? Who gave them their gifts? Who created music itself and the ability to perform it? All that is admirable and fascinating in human beings comes from their creator." [5]

"It's not God who's boring; it's us. Did we invent wit and humor and laughter? No, God did. We'll never begin to exhaust God's sense of humor and His love for adventure. The real question is this: 'How could God not be bored with us?'" [6]

Because God is not boring, neither will heaven be.

Heaven Will Not Be Boring
Because You Will Not
Be Boring (1 Corinthians 15:51–52)

We can imagine that God is not boring, but it may take a bit more faith to imagine that we ourselves will not be boring for eternity. Here's the reason we won't be: We're going to be changed. First Corinthians 15:51–52 says—twice—that "we shall all be changed." And in Philippians 3:20–21, Paul says that our "lowly body" will be "conformed to His glorious body."

So, that makes it easier to understand. We get down on ourselves in this life, thinking we are not the most scintillating of characters—and that may be true. But we will be different people in heaven, having been conformed to the image of Jesus Christ (Romans 8:29).

Joseph Bayly wrote a book about death called *The View from a Hearse* in which he said, "It must also be remembered that before believers live in heaven, they will experience radical change. A fetus in the womb is not ready for the earth until he goes through the radical change called birth. Until that change takes place, he cannot enjoy life in the new world . . . . The believer will be changed. God has promised it. Let us not therefore prejudge or question God about things we do not fully understand on this side of that promised change." [7]

Now, we've removed God and ourselves from the possible causes for heaven being boring. But what about the rest of the population of heaven? Won't they be boring?

HEAVEN WILL NOT BE BORING BECAUSE YOUR FRIENDS WILL NOT BE BORING (HEBREWS 12:22-23)

The book of Hebrews tells us we are on our way to the "heavenly Jerusalem," the location of the "spirits of just men made perfect." Now who is being referred to with that statement? It is none other than the Old Testament saints. In fact, positionally speaking, we are already seated with them in the heavenly places. Hebrews 12 also says we will join an "innumerable company of angels" and "the general assembly and church of the firstborn who are registered in heaven."

So we are going to spend eternity in the company of angels, the Old Testament saints, and the population of the entire church of Jesus Christ. Heaven is going to be the most exciting place you could possibly imagine.

Even at our best here on earth, we sometimes wonder about people's motives and meanings. But in heaven, there will be none of that. There will be complete honesty, openness, and vulnerability to one another. Fear, ulterior motives, manipulation—all the things that separate us from one another on earth will be gone. In fact, it's hard even to imagine such an environment because we're so used to our flawed way of life here on earth.

Think about the opportunity to fellowship with saints from previous eras of history. People we might have been friends with a thousand years ago, but couldn't because we lived at a different time, will become our friends! And think about getting to know people like Abraham, Moses, Joshua, David, Daniel, Peter, Stephen, and the apostle Paul. And what about the opportunity to have a meal with C. S. Lewis, Charles Spurgeon, and missionaries like Hudson Taylor and Jim Elliot.

Are you bored yet? If you stop and spend a moment thinking about what it is actually going to be like when we get to heaven, boredom will be the last thought in your mind. I don't think most Christians have actually stopped to think about the realities that await us there.

HEAVEN WILL NOT BE BORING BECAUSE YOUR WORK WILL NOT BE BORING (REVELATION 7:15)

The fourth reason heaven won't be boring is that our work will keep us so busy and interested, we won't have time to be bored.

Throughout the book of Revelation, we get glimpses of the service that is taking place there at all times. Whether we will be involved in those same kinds of service or not, I don't know (Revelation 7:3, 15; 11:18; 15:3; 19:5; 22:3, 6). But I am confident there is going to be work (service) for us to perform. Service implies servants, and servants have tasks to perform and responsibilities to carry out. I don't think Christ is going to say to us, "Well done, good and faithful servant—take the rest of eternity off." Jesus said, "Well done, good and faithful servant; you were faithful over a few things, I will make you ruler over many things. Enter into the joy of your lord" (Matthew 25:21). That sounds like we're going to be given "many things" to do in heaven.

For the first thousand years during the Millennium, we're going to rule with Christ over the renewed earth, which will undoubtedly involve tasks of service. Imagine being a "civil servant" in the government of which Christ is the head—for a thousand years. All of us will be given service to perform that completely matches our capacity and desires—work that will leave us ready for more.

In his book, *The Biblical Doctrine of Heaven*, Wilbur Smith wrote, "In heaven we will be permitted to finish many of (these) worthy tasks which we had dreamed to do while on (this) earth but which . . . neither had time nor ability…" (to accomplish).[8]

Randy Alcorn raises these interesting questions about our work in heaven: "What will it be like (in heaven) to perform a task, to build and create, knowing that what we're doing will last forever and ever? What will it be like to always be gaining skills so that our best work will always be ahead of us? Because our minds and bodies will never fade and because we will never lack resources and opportunity, our work won't degenerate. Buildings won't last for only fifty years, and books won't be in print for only twenty years. They'll last forever" and ever and ever.[9]

In short, everything we do in heaven will have eternity stamped all over it. I have a feeling there will be work to do, perhaps throughout the universe, that we can't even comprehend.

HEAVEN WILL NOT BE BORING BECAUSE HEAVEN IS THE PLACE YOU'VE ALWAYS LONGED FOR (ROMANS 8:22–23)

Paul gives us these powerful words in the eighth chapter of Romans: "For we know that the whole creation groans and labors with birth pangs together until now. Not only that, but we also who have the firstfruits of the Spirit, even we ourselves groan within ourselves, eagerly waiting for the adoption, the redemption of our body."

Paul is saying that, within every Christian, there is a hunger that is waiting to be fulfilled. It's as if we know there is something that is missing from our redemption experience, that the last chapter has yet to be revealed. It's what Ecclesiastes 3:11 refers to with regard to the "eternity" God has put in our hearts. It's something that can only be satisfied by heaven; nothing on earth can fill the eternity-shaped void in our hearts.

Mark Buchanan expressed it this way: "Here is the surprise. God has made us this way. He made us to yearn—to always be hungry for something we can't get, to always be missing something we can't find, to always be disappointed with what we receive, to always have an insatiable emptiness that no thing can fill, and an untamable restlessness that no discovery can still. Yearning itself is healthy—a kind of compass inside us, pointing (us toward) True North."[10]

Often men and women in the workforce strive to achieve a certain goal or to get a promotion to the next level in their careers. Once they finally make it to the proverbial "corner office," they sit down behind their big new desk and realize it wasn't all they thought it would be. And they think there's something wrong with them. In fact, that's quite normal! There is nothing on this earth that will ever satisfy us completely. We were created for the perfection of heaven and will never be satisfied until we arrive there. So if there is an itch you can't seem to get scratched here on earth, don't worry—that just means your compass is still pointing you toward heaven.

C. S. Lewis expressed our dissatisfaction this way: "Creatures are not born with desires unless satisfaction for those desires exists. A baby feels hunger: Well, there's such a thing as food. A duckling wants to swim: Well, there is such a thing as water. Men feel sexual desire: Well, there is such a thing as sex. If I find in myself a desire which no experience in this world can satisfy, the most probable explanation is that I was made for another world. (And) if none of my earthly pleasures satisfy it, that does not mean that the universe is a fraud . . . earthly pleasures were never meant to satisfy it, but only to arouse it, (and) to suggest the real thing." [11]

When I get to heaven, that ache is going to go away. When I get to heaven, everything I do will bring me absolute, perfect satisfaction, reward, fulfillment, and joy. When I get to heaven, I will never engage in anything that leaves me feeling even a tad bit empty. The reason you aren't going to be bored in heaven is that heaven is everything you've been looking for.

If you think heaven is going to be disappointing in some way, remember the truth of 2 Thessalonians 1:9: "These shall be punished with everlasting destruction from the presence of the Lord and from the glory of His power." Consider being shut outside the gates of heaven for all eternity!

Have you made sure that the promise of heaven is yours? It's not arrogant for you to say "Yes." It is simply your confidence in the promises of God. Jesus said He was going to prepare a place for you, that where He is you may be also. If you believe Him, and have trusted Him as your Savior from sin, then heaven is yours. Get ready—it's going to be grand, forever!

Notes:

1. Quoted in: James T. Jeremiah, *A Place Called Heaven* (El Cajon: Turning Point for God, 2005), 45.

2. Viktor Frankl, *Man's Search for Meaning* (Boston: Beacon Press, 2000).

3. http://www.brainyquote.com/quotes/quotes/i/isaacasimo122403.html

4. John Eldredge, *The Journey of Desire: Searching for the Life We've Only Dreamed Of* (Nashville: Nelson, 2000), 111.

5. Randy Alcorn, *Heaven* (Wheaton: Tyndale House Publishers, 2004), 184.

6. Ibid, 394–395.

7. Joseph Bayly, *The View from a Hearse* (Elgin: Cook Publishing, 1969), 87–91.

8. Wilbur M. Smith, *The Biblical Doctrine of Heaven* (Chicago: Moody Press, 1968), 195.

9. Alcorn, op. cit., 398.

10. Mark Buchanan, *Things Unseen* (Sisters: Multnomah, 2002).

11. C. S. Lewis, *Mere Christianity* (New York: Macmillan, 1960), 120.

1. There are two dimensions to the Christian's resurrection life experience: the Millennium and heaven itself.

   a. When Christ returns to establish His millennial kingdom, who returns with Him? (Revelation 19:14)

   b. Of whom are the "armies of heaven" made? (Revelation 19:14; see Matthew 25:31)

   c. Based on what they are wearing, who might make up these "armies"? (Revelation 19:7-8)

   d. Based on Revelation 17:14, who will be helping the Lord to defeat the Antichrist? (Revelation 17:13-14)

   e. Do these future roles for resurrected saints sound boring or exciting to you?

2. Based on what you know of the lives of the original 12 disciples, would you call their lives boring or exciting? Give some examples to illustrate your choice.

   a. When a leader lives an exciting life, are the lives of his followers usually exciting or boring? What would you anticipate your life to be like as a follower of Christ in the Millennium?

   b. Describe the job that Christ told the original disciples they would have when He returned to reign on earth. (Matthew 19:28)

   c. What exciting role is promised to "him who overcomes" in Revelation 3:21?

   d. What role do 2 Timothy 2:2 and Revelation 20:4, 6 suggest for Christians during the Millennium?

   e. How exciting does Romans 8:17 make the future sound for believers?

3. How many "elders" did John see in his vision of heaven? (Revelation 4:4)

   a. Some have suggested that "24" symbolically represents all believers from the Old and New Testament eras: 12 for the 12 _____ of Israel and 12 for the 12_____ of Jesus.

   b. What do the thrones in Revelation 4:4 suggest? (Compare with 2 Timothy 2:12 and Revelation 20:4, 6)

   c. If the elders represent believers, does that kind of proximity to the throne of God (Revelation 4:10) sound boring or exciting?

4. What do you most anticipate about life in heaven?

DID YOU KNOW?

The Bible mentions only two individuals who went to heaven without dying first: Enoch and Elijah. Enoch "enjoyed a close relationship with God throughout his life [365 years]. Then suddenly, he disappeared because God took him" (Genesis 5:24, *NLT*). Hebrews 11:5 says that Enoch "did not see death." Elijah was walking and talking with his protégé Elisha when "suddenly a chariot of fire and horses of fire appeared and separated the two of them, and Elijah went up to heaven in a whirlwind" (2 Kings 2:11 NIV). Their transition to immortality was not through the normal portals of death and bodily resurrection.

THE ULTIMATE "EXTREME MAKEOVER"

1 Corinthians 15:35–49

In this lesson we discover the nature of the believer's resurrection body.

OUTLINE

Much speculation has been offered about what those who populate heaven will look like. Will they appear as angels? As "ghosts"? The Bible makes it clear that believers will have corporeal bodies that are recognizable, but which are free from all the limitations of bodies on planet earth.

I. **The Requirement of Resurrection Is the Death of the Body**

II. **The Result of Resurrection Is a Different Kind of Body**
   A. Our New Bodies Will Be Indestructible
   B. Our New Bodies Will Be Identifiable
      1. Jesus Said That His Body Was Real
      2. Jesus Ate on at Least Two Occasions
      3. Jesus Told Thomas to Touch His Body
      4. Jesus Told Mary Not to Hold on to Him
   C. Our New Bodies Will Be Incredible
   D. Our New Bodies Will Be Infinite

In the spirit of previous lessons, here is another epitaph, this time from Benjamin Franklin, that ties in perfectly with the message of this lesson:

"[Benjamin Franklin] . . . lies in the grave like the cover of an old book, with its contents torn out, stripped of its lettering, but which will appear once again in a new and more eloquent edition, revised and corrected by the author."[1]

Those words eloquently describe the ultimate "extreme makeover" every Christian will one day receive from God. In 1 Corinthians 15, Paul deals with the doctrine of the resurrection—both the resurrection of Christ and of the believer. As part of that doctrine, he talks about the change that will occur in our physical bodies when we are resurrected at the end of this age.

THE REQUIREMENT OF RESURRECTION IS THE DEATH OF THE BODY (1 CORINTHIANS 15:36)

There is a prerequisite for having a resurrection body: First you have to have a dead body! I think Paul is having a little fun with the Corinthians when he says, "Foolish one, what you sow is not made alive unless it dies" (verse 36).

Here Paul is obviously picking up on the teaching of Jesus who said in John 12:24, "Most assuredly, I say to you, unless a grain of wheat falls into the ground and dies, it remains alone; but if it dies, it produces much grain."

The biblical perspective on death is different from the world's. Death is to be embraced, not feared. Death is the precursor to the wonderful resurrection body God has planned for the believer. If we did not die, we would be stuck with our current body for all eternity. Paul strikes a positive note right up front, saying that death is not to be feared. It's what has to occur before we can be changed. Without death there is no resurrection.

THE RESULT OF RESURRECTION IS A DIFFERENT KIND OF BODY (1 CORINTHIANS 15:37–38)

In the next two verses, Paul makes an important point: The seed is one thing, the body of the plant it produces is another. In other words, sow one shape or form and reap another—a kernel of corn is radically different from the tall, green stalk that emerges from the earth. Applied to the human body, the body that dies and is buried in the earth is raised as a totally different kind of body. On the day of our resurrection, the body that comes out of the ground will be very different from the body that went into the ground.

Paul gives us four ways in which the bodies that come out of the ground will be different from the bodies that were buried in the ground.

Our New Bodies Will Be Indestructible (verse 42)

There has only been one body that was perfect—incorruptible—and that was the body of Jesus Christ. This was prophesied by the psalmist who wrote, ". . . nor will You allow Your Holy One to see corruption" (Psalm 16:10). Our bodies, however, are "sown [buried] in corruption."

Our present bodies get old, wear out, and eventually die. Things stop working like they once did, all part of the aging process of "corruptible" bodies. Despite the claims of science, there is nothing that will ever grant us immortality on this earth. On the other hand, our resurrected bodies will be incorruptible—they will last forever! They will not age, wear out, or be susceptible to disease.

I ride a bike now for exercise, and I have learned that it is much easier to go with the wind than against it. But that won't be true in heaven because my resurrection body will not get tired, strained, or become short of breath. Our bodies will be perfect in every way—indestructible!

Our New Bodies Will Be Identifiable (verse 43)

Second, we are not going to be ghost-like apparitions that all look the same. Our new bodies will be identifiable. Paul says our new bodies will be "raised in glory," which literally means "brilliance."

I don't know if we're going to have a brilliant "glow" or not. We have to look at Philippians 3:20–21 to get an idea of what Paul is probably talking about here. There Paul says that our "lowly body" will be conformed to Christ's "glorious body." Our new bodies will be like the body of the Lord Jesus Christ. The apostle John wrote that "It has not yet been revealed what we shall be, but we know that when He is revealed, we shall be like Him, for we shall see Him as He is" (1 John 3:2). Paul concludes this thought in verse 49 of 1 Corinthians 15 by saying, "And as we have borne the image of the man of dust [Adam], we shall also bear the image of the heavenly Man [Christ]."

The best glimpse we have of what Jesus' glorified body was like (and thus what our resurrected bodies will be like) is in the forty-day period between His resurrection and ascension. We can identify five characteristics of His body during that period:

1. Jesus Said That His Body Was Real (Luke 24:39)

   Jesus, when He met with the disciples after His resurrection, invited them to touch Him to see that His body was real: "Handle me and see, for a spirit does not have flesh and bones as you see I have." Jesus had a physical, corporeal body after His resurrection from the dead.

2. Jesus Ate on at Least Two Occasions (Luke 24:42–43; John 21:12–13)

   People ask me this question about heaven more than any other: "Are we going to eat in heaven?" Apparently so, since Jesus ate in his post resurrection body. He ate a piece of fish and some honeycomb on one occasion (Luke 24), and (apparently) shared fish and bread with His disciples on the shores of the Sea of Galilee (John 21).

   It seems that the role of food changes from being a necessity to a pleasure. We won't need to eat to stay alive because our bodies will be incorruptible. But we will enjoy the pleasure of eating just as Adam and Eve would have done in the Garden of Eden before they sinned.

3. Jesus Told Thomas to Touch His Body (John 20:27)

   When Thomas doubted that Jesus had really been raised from the dead, Jesus encouraged him to reach out and touch His wounds, to see that it was really Jesus in the body in which He had been crucified.

4. Jesus Told Mary Not to Hold on to Him (John 20:17)

   When Mary encountered Jesus in the garden after His resurrection, He cautioned her not to cling to Him—to throw her arms around Him. He would not have said that had it not been possible for her to cling to Him; that is, if His body had not been a true physical body.

So, if our bodies are going to be like Jesus' body, we will be physical, we will be recognizable, we will be able to eat, and we'll be able to communicate. Jesus was as recognizable and communicable after His resurrection as He was before His death. Paul says in 1 Corinthians 13:12, "Now I know in part, but then I shall know just as I also am known." In heaven, we will know and be known.

On the Mount of Transfiguration, Moses and Elijah were recognized by the disciples (Matthew 17:1–4), and Jesus said that in the kingdom "many will come from east and west, and sit down with Abraham, Isaac, and Jacob in the kingdom of heaven" (Matthew 8:11). It would be hard to sit down with Abraham if you couldn't tell who he was!

Our New Bodies Will Be Incredible (1 Corinthians 15:43b)

Paul says our bodies are sown in weakness (death is the ultimate weakness), but "raised in power." When we come out of the grave, we will come out as power personified. The weakness we experience now will be a thing of our past life.

When a group from our church went to Africa on a missions trip, we experienced just what physical weakness is all about. Our task was to work in the vegetable gardens that were being planted as a source of food for African villagers. We went out strong in the morning; but when we returned in the evening, we looked bad!— like we'd been run over by a truck. The work was hard; and as the week wore on, our stamina decreased markedly. In this life we simply do not have the power we need to do all we would like to do.

On one occasion after His resurrection, Jesus just appeared in a room where the disciples were. He didn't use the door—He was just there (John 20:19). Will we have that same kind of power in our resurrected bodies—the ability to transport ourselves from one place to another? To the degree that we are like Jesus in His resurrected body, I would think so, though we can't know for sure.

The point is that we can't even imagine what it will be like to live in bodies that are not limited as our current physical bodies are. Jesus was not constrained by the limitations of His earthly body, and neither will we be in the resurrection.

Our Bodies Will Be Infinite (1 Corinthians 15:44)

Finally, Paul draws a distinction between a natural body and a spiritual one. In this passage, he points to Adam as the image, bearer for our natural body and to Christ, the last Adam, as the image bearer for the spiritual body we will receive.

What is a "spiritual" body? First, Paul doesn't mean it is an immaterial body. We've already seen that Jesus had a physical body, and so will we—a body that can be touched and felt. Instead, a spiritual body is one that is not controlled by the physical appetites of the fallen, carnal human nature. Instead, our bodies will be spiritual, controlled by the Holy Spirit. The basic difference between natural bodies and spiritual bodies is that one is at home on the earth, and the other is at home in heaven. That's why Paul says our natural bodies cannot inherit the kingdom of God (1 Corinthians 15:50).

Our current bodies are completely unsuited for heaven, which is why God will give us new ones when we are resurrected from the dead. Our spiritual bodies will welcome the control of the Spirit, and we will no longer have to contend with the flesh. If you have ever had a brief period of time, even just a few moments, where you felt completely in step with the Spirit of God, you have tasted heaven. It will be a time when our desires and the desires of God are one. There will be no conflict, no competition between Spirit and flesh. Our whole desire will be to do the will of God. Watch for those moments in this life and, when they happen, remind yourself that you are headed for an eternity of such bliss if you know Jesus as your Savior.

So Paul summarizes the order of events in verses 51 and 52: Some will be alive when Christ comes, and some will be "asleep," having already died. But all will be changed in a moment of time when the last trumpet sounds and the dead are raised and changed from corruption into incorruption.

From 1 Thessalonians 4, we can add the specific order of the changes that will take place. The dead in Christ will rise first; then those who are alive when Christ returns will join them in the air, and all will be changed. Instantaneously—"in the twinkling of an eye" (1 Corinthians 15:52)—our corruptible, natural, weak, and limited bodies will become incorruptible, spiritual, powerful, and limitless bodies.

I sincerely hope I am alive when that happens—when Christ returns for His church at the Rapture. I believe we ought to all have that longing and hope, to hear the trumpet and the archangel's shout, to see our Savior in the clouds, and to experience the transformation of our bodies. What a glorious moment to live for! What a blessed hope we have, to know that whether we are alive or not when He comes, we shall all be changed!

Joni Eareckson Tada is one of many saints who have experienced physical disabilities and limitations in this life, and she has written beautifully about her hope and God's promise for a new body: "I still can hardly believe it, I, with shriveled, bent fingers, atrophied muscles, gnarled knees, and no feeling from the shoulders down, will one day have a new body, light, bright, and clothed in right-eousness—powerful and dazzling. Can you imagine the hope this gives someone spinal cord injured like me? Or someone who is cerebral palsied, brain-injured, or (who) has multiple sclerosis? Imagine the hope this gives someone who is manic-depressive. No other religion, no other philosophy promises new bodies, new hearts and minds. Only in the Gospel of Christ do hurting people find such incredible hope."[2]

No wonder Paul said that if in this life only we have hope, we are most miserable (1 Corinthians 15:19 KJV). But we have hope beyond this life. And that hope is in Jesus. One day all of the pains and the aches and the deformities and the deficiencies that we carry in our earthly bodies are going to be taken away when we get our heavenly bodies. We will know the joy of living in the perfection and glory that God intended for us from the beginning.

This truth about our new physical bodies is not the least of the reasons I am passionate about taking people to heaven with me. I don't want anyone to miss what God has planned for those who are His.

The reality of a new body is part of the expectation of glory that heaven represents. Since we have never lived in perfect, limitless, spiritual bodies, it's very difficult to imagine what it will be like. The surest way to find out is to experience the change yourself by being one of those Christ calls to Himself when He comes for His own. Make sure you have entrusted yourself to Him by faith and that you enter eternity with your ultimate "extreme makeover"!

Notes:
1. http://sln.fi.edu/franklin/timeline/epitaph.html
2. Joni Eareckson Tada, *Heaven: Your Real Home* (Grand Rapids: Zondervan, 1955), 53.

1. Read 2 Corinthians 5:1-10.

   a. What metaphor does Paul use to describe our earthly body? (verse 1a)

   b. What is waiting for us when our earthly sojourn is finished? (verse 1b)

   c. What is implied in verse 2 concerning the difference between earthly life ("groan") and heavenly life?

   d. What is the meaning of verse 3 concerning our heavenly existence? (To what does "naked" refer?) Will we be "spirits" or corporeal bodies in heaven?

   e. Who did the Old Testament saints see doing the "swallowing" in this life? (verse 4; see Psalm 69:15; Proverbs 1:12)

   f. How did Paul reverse that image in verse 4? That is, in the age following the resurrection of Jesus, who does the "swallowing"?

g. What guarantee have we been given that death is going to be "swallowed up by life"? (verse 5; see Ephesians 1:13)

h. What tension does the Christian live with while on earth? (verse 6)

i. Since we have never seen heaven or our new heavenly bodies, what is the basis of the Christian's hope? (verse 7)

j. Given a choice, where would the Christian rather be? (verse 8)

k. In either place, what is the Christian's highest priority? (verse 9)

l. What motivates our desire to be well-pleasing to the Lord? (verse 10; see also 1 Corinthians 3:11-15)

2. Read John 20:16-17, 24-28.

   a. What is the implication of Jesus' words to Mary concerning the nature of His resurrection body? (verse 17) (Is it possible to "cling to" a spirit?)

   b. Same question—this time for Thomas. What physical evidence did Jesus offer Thomas of His resurrection? (verse 27)

   c. What does Paul say must happen to you before you can enter heaven? (1 Corinthians 15:50-54).

   d. What assurance do Christians have that they will put on a heavenly body? (1 Corinthians 15:20).

DID YOU KNOW?

Several resurrections from the dead were recorded in the New Testament. Jesus raised the deceased son of a widow from the dead (Luke 7:11-15), as well as His friend Lazarus (John 11:38-44). He also brought the daughter of Jairus, a synagogue ruler, back to life (Mark 5:22-24). The apostle Peter raised a young man named Eutychus from the dead in Troas (Acts 20:7-12). The bodies of those raised from the dead were not, however, "resurrection bodies"— mortality putting on immortality (1 Corinthians 15:53-54). Each of those raised from the dead died a second time later in their lives to await their immortal resurrection bodies.

HEAVEN'S OSCARS

Selected Scriptures

In this lesson we learn about the rewards believers will receive in heaven.

OUTLINE

Athletes in ancient Greece practiced for years to win prizes that would soon fade away. Christians who run the spiritual race diligently will receive rewards for their faithfulness at the judgment seat of Christ, rewards which they will reinvest in the glory of Christ for eternity.

I. **The Day of Heaven's Rewards**

II. **The Distinction of Heaven's Rewards**

III. **The Description of Heaven's Rewards**
   A. The Victor's Crown
   B. The Crown of Rejoicing
   C. The Crown of Righteousness
   D. The Crown of Life
   E. The Crown of Glory

IV. **The Difference Heaven's Rewards Can Make**
   A. Remember That the Lord Himself Is Your Chief Reward
   B. Resist Doing Works Outwardly for the Purpose of Receiving a Reward
   C. Reflect Upon the Ultimate Goal of Any Rewards We May Receive

To continue our theme of heaven-oriented epitaphs, here's an interesting one found on the tombstone of a woman named Samantha:

"Here lies the body of Samantha Proctor
She catched a cold and wouldn't doctor.
She couldn't stay. She had to go.
Praise God from whom all blessings flow."

I did a little research and discovered forty-two different awards shows that are available to be seen each year. There are the Academy Awards, the People's Choice Awards, the Golden Globe Awards, the Screen Actors Guild Awards, the Grammy Awards, the Country Music Association Awards—and the list goes on and on. But there is an awards show coming that this world knows nothing of, one that will put all other award shows to shame for its grandeur and the quality of the awards to be given. Those are the rewards given to believers prior to their permanent entrance into heaven.

Some people don't understand the rationale behind Christians getting rewards. They think it sounds like bribing children to be good by offering them candy. Doing and being good, they say, should be their own reward. But the idea of rewards is completely biblical and consistent with God's character as we will see in this lesson.

The concept of rewards is found in the Old Testament (Psalm 58:11; 62:12), and Jesus opens the New Testament era by citing rewards for those persecuted for the sake of righteousness (Matthew 5:11–12). And at the end of the Bible, in Revelation 22:12, we find Jesus saying, "And behold, I am coming quickly, and My reward is with Me . . . ." Rewards are mentioned in many other places in the New Testament: Mark 9:41; 10:29–30; Luke 18:29–30; 1 Corinthians 3:14; Colossians 3:24; Hebrews 6:10–12.

In this lesson, we'll look at the timing and the kinds of rewards God intends to give as part of our entrance into heaven.

THE DAY OF HEAVEN'S REWARDS

Here's the big picture: The Bible says that after all believers, dead and alive, are removed from earth at the Rapture of the church, believers will be judged individually for their works as Christians; and special rewards will be handed out. Here are excerpts from several Scriptures that address this event:

- Romans 14:12: "So then each of us shall give account of himself to God.

- 2 Corinthians 5:10: "For we must all appear before the judgment seat of Christ."
- Ephesians 6:8: "Knowing that whatever good anyone does, he will receive the same from the Lord."
- 1 Corinthians 3:11–15: "If anyone's work which he has built on it endures, he will receive a reward."

This judgment has nothing to do with our salvation. Rather it has to do with the kind of Christian we have been, a judgment of our faithfulness as followers of Christ. The penetrating gaze of Christ will look past all our posturing and spin and see us for what we really are. There'll be no excuses or rationalizations. We will stand silently before the Son of God and know that His judgment is wholly true. Whatever rewards we receive (or not) will be totally appropriate. There will be no need for appeals or discussions since His judgments will be perfect.

THE DISTINCTION OF HEAVEN'S REWARDS

The Judgment Seat of Christ is not a final exam to determine your suitability for heaven. Because this judgment does evaluate our works, some have thought it was to determine whether we have enough good works to merit entrance into heaven. That is wrong. The Bible could not be more clear that we are saved by grace, not according to our works (Ephesians 2:8–9; see also Romans 8:1; 1 Corinthians 15:3; 1 John 2:12). If you have trusted Jesus Christ as your Savior, your sins have been forgiven; and that is what qualifies you to enter the holy presence of God in heaven. Your sins—past, present, and future— were paid for on Calvary's cross and will not be a matter of examination at the Judgment Seat of Christ regarding your salvation.

Instead, the Judgment Seat of Christ is where you will be rewarded for your service to the Lord in your Christian experience. This service is a matter of faithfulness on the part of those who are already saved, not works that bear on your salvation. These are the works described in Ephesians 2:10 that follow after our salvation by grace: "For we are His workmanship, created in Christ Jesus for good works, which God prepared beforehand that we should walk in them."

We are not saved by good works, but are saved for good works. This truth has apparently not registered with much of the Christian community since surveys indicate the lifestyles of most Christians are not significantly different from non-Christians. There will be a rude awakening at the Judgment Seat of Christ when many discover there are no rewards given to them.

Bruce Wilkinson has summarized the difference between being saved and being rewarded for service: "Our eternal destination is the consequence of what we believe on earth. Our eternal compensation is the consequence of how we behave on earth."[1]

When you stand before the Judgment Seat of Christ, it's not about getting into heaven. You'll already be there! It's about heaven's evaluation of your faithful service to Christ. The prospect of this coming judgment is what should keep us from judging one another in this life. We are not the judge—Christ is.

THE DESCRIPTION OF HEAVEN'S REWARDS

The New Testament describes five different kinds of rewards, referred to as crowns, that will be given to believers. I do not believe these are all the rewards that will be given, but are representative of the whole range of crowns that will be handed out.

The Victor's Crown (1 Corinthians 9:25–27)

The victor's crown is called an "imperishable crown" by Paul and is compared to the perishable wreaths for which athletes competed in the Greek games. There were two athletic festivals in Greece, the Olympic Games and the Isthmian Games, the latter being held at Corinth. Contestants trained vigorously for ten months, and Paul used this training to illustrate the discipline necessary for spiritual success.

Paul's point is that winning requires discipline and training. If athletes worked diligently for months to win a perishable wreath of olive branches, how much more diligently should we work to win an imperishable crown from God?

Training requires the ability to say "No" when necessary—and not just to things that are sinful. As the saying goes, "The good is the enemy of the best." In order to be and do our best for God, it may require choosing to focus only on those things with the highest value in an eternal sense. There are lots of "good" and "better" things in life that can take our focus off the "best," and it is up to us to identify them and choose accordingly. Bible study, evangelism, helping a neighbor in the name of Christ, sacrificing personal desires to free up money for God's work—all of these choices require sacrifice. And when that kind of discipline is exercised, the Victor's Crown is given.

Think of the difference between an athlete and a non-athlete, to continue Paul's illustration. An athlete makes everything subservient to his goal of winning. The non-athlete lets other desires—food, sleep, possessions—take precedence. The spiritual life is no different. Our willingness to submit to the goal of fulfilling Christ's commands will characterize us as a "Victor"—one who strives to win the race. Our goal is to consider our spiritual walk like an athlete considers a race—something to make sacrifices for in order to win.

The Crown of Rejoicing *(1 Thessalonians 2:19)*

Paul asked the Thessalonian Christians, "For what is our hope, or joy, or crown of rejoicing?" And his answer is startling: "Is it not even you in the presence of our Lord Jesus Christ at His coming?"

This crown is given to those who are responsible for others standing before Christ at His return—often called the soul-winner's crown. It's the reward given to those who reach out beyond themselves to lead others to heaven.

Christians talk about Jesus to each other often, and that's good. But when is the last time you talked about Jesus to someone who isn't a Christian? Paul's love for the Thessalonians is evident in his two letters for them—they were his hope, his joy, his crown of rejoicing.

The Crown of Righteousness *(2 Timothy 4:8)*

Paul writes the words in this verse in the last days of his life. He is a prisoner in Rome and knows his days are numbered. But he is content, knowing he has run the race with faithfulness. He looks forward to receiving the crown of righteousness that is given "to all who have loved His appearing"—those who have eagerly anticipated the second coming of Christ.

Many Christians are so caught up with all the "exciting" things they're involved in on earth that they have forgotten that earth is not their home. They love their life here and have many places to go, things to do, and people to see before going to heaven. This crown is not for those believers. It is for those who long for heaven, their true home, who long to see the face of their Savior when He comes for them in the clouds.

The Crown of Life *(James 1:12; Revelation 2:10)*

The recipients of this crown are those "who love Him," even, as Revelation says, in the face of death. It is a crown given to those who maintain their love for Christ while enduring and triumphing over persecution and temptation, even martyrdom. Think of the number of Christians we will see wearing this crown in heaven because they gave their life for the sake of Christ throughout the centuries of church history.

But it's not just martyrs who will receive this crown—it's any who have suffered, endured, persevered, and encouraged others to do so as well, those who have kept the faith when it was costly to do so.

I wonder if the great hymn writer Charles Wesley had this crown in mind when he wrote these words:

In hope of that immortal crown,
I now the cross sustain
And gladly wander up and down,
And smile at toil and pain:
I suffer out my three-score years,
Till my Deliverer come,
And wipe away His servant's tears,
And take His exile home.

The crown of life—an "immortal crown" given to those who have smiled "at toil and pain" 'til their Deliverer came.

The Crown of Glory (1 Peter 5:4)

This is a crown I get excited about because it is given to those who are faithful shepherds of the people of God. But it's not just for pastors, elders, deacons, and leaders with visibility in the church. It will be for all those who were shepherds of the sheep at some level—small groups, Sunday school classes, ministry teams, and in other places of ministry. The wounds of sheep continually need to be bound up, and they need to be guided and encouraged along the way. The crown of glory is for those who lay down their lives in that calling of leadership.

THE DIFFERENCE HEAVEN'S REWARDS CAN MAKE

Now that we know what the five crowns are that are mentioned in the New Testament, what should we do with this knowledge? What difference should these future rewards make in our present-day relationship with the Lord?

Remember That the Lord Himself Is Your Chief Reward

In Genesis 15:1, we find God making this statement to Abram: "Do not be afraid, Abram. I am your shield, your exceedingly great reward." God was making great promises to Abram in those days about his future, and it would have been possible to be both fearful of the future and prideful about the blessings God was going to bestow. But God reminds Abram that He, God, is Abram's true reward. Land and descendants and blessing would be nothing apart from God in His life.

Resist Doing Works Outwardly for the Purpose of Receiving a Reward

There is enough of the flesh left in us to be tempted, like an immature child, to be obedient for the purpose of gaining a reward. That kind of insincere play-acting drew some strong words from Jesus when He saw it in the religious community of His day: "Take heed that you do not do your charitable deeds before men, to be seen by them. Otherwise you have no reward from your Father in heaven" (Matthew 6:1). He went on to say that our good deeds ought to be done in secret if we want God the Father to reward us for them.

If we are serving the Lord only to get a reward, we have totally misunderstood Christianity. Our motive for serving should be the same as His motive for saving: LOVE! Rewards are simply God's expressions of joy in response to our love for Him. I have never heard anyone say that they are serving God wholeheartedly in order that they can get a great reward when they get to heaven. Because that is a self-serving notion, you couldn't be serving the Lord while thinking that way.

Reflect Upon the Ultimate Goal of Any Rewards We May Receive

Finally, and most important, we need to stay continually aware of what we will ultimately do with the crowns we receive in heaven. We read in Revelation 4:10–11 that the 24 elders, who represent the church in heaven, "cast their crowns before the throne, saying: 'You are worthy, O Lord, to receive glory and honor and power; for You created all things, and by Your will they exist and were created.'"

After we receive our crowns as rewards in heaven, we're going to be so excited about the privilege of having served Jesus that we're going to fall down at His feet and offer them back to Him as offerings of worship and praise. He gave His best to bring us to heaven, and we'll offer our best back to Him for the privilege of being there.

Don't miss out on that amazing experience. Live wholeheartedly for Christ for the rest of your life so you will have a crown to cast at His feet.

Note:

1. Bruce Wilkinson, *A Life God Rewards: Why Everything You Do Today Matters Forever* (Sisters: Multnomah Press, 2002).

APPLICATION

1. The "harvest principle" of Galatians 6:7 governs all human activity and God's response. What does this principle state?

   a. What is God's eternal response to man? Read Romans 6:20-23. (Those who have been set free receive_____ . For the lost, the wages of sin is _____ .)

   b. How are those rewards experienced in this life, before eternity? (Galatians 6:8)

2. Read Romans 2:1-11.

   a. What is the overriding message of verses 1-3 concerning judgment? (Is there anyone who will escape God's judgment?)

   b. What does the postponement of God's judgment demonstrate about Him? (verse 4a)

   c. What is the postponement of judgment supposed to accomplish in us? (verse 4b)

   d. What are those who refuse to repent "treasuring up" for themselves? (verse 5)

e. What is God's principle employed in all judgment? (Galatians 6:7; verse 6)

f. What will those who do good receive as a reward? (verses 7, 10)

g. What will the disobedient receive as a reward? (verses 8-9)

h. How do we know there is no impartiality with God? (verses 10b-11) (What other categories of humans are there besides Jews and Gentiles?)

i. How do you reconcile Romans 2:7, 10 with Romans 3:10-18? In other words, has anyone ever done good enough to receive a righteous reward?

j. So how do those who want to do good (but often fail) ever receive a righteous reward? (Romans 3:22-23).

3. Christians will still be judged in spite of having received a righteous reward freely. What will be the basis of their judgment? (1 Corinthians 3:11-13)

   a. If Christians' works survive the judgment, what will happen? (verse 14)

   b. If their work doesn't survive the judgment, what will happen to them and their work? (verse 15)

DID YOU KNOW?

The Romans used a "judgment seat" (Greek *bema*) for dispensing judgments at trials or for making official pronouncements. Pontius Pilate sat down on a *bema* at the "trial" of Jesus in Jerusalem (Matthew 27:19), and Paul was brought before the judgment seat of Gallio in Corinth (Acts 18:12). Herod delivered a speech in Caesarea from the *bema* (Acts 12:21), the same one used by Festus when he interrogated Paul years later (Acts 25:6). The idea of the *bema* as a place of judgment for Christians was used twice by Paul, calling it "the judgment seat of Christ" (Romans 14:10; 2 Corinthians 5:10).

THE HEAVENLY CITY

Revelation 21

In this lesson we discover the glory of the New Jerusalem, our heavenly home.

OUTLINE

Parts of heaven are like folklore—"streets of gold," "pearly gates," and the like. But the city called the New Jerusalem is not fable or fancy; it is a literal city that will be the eternal capital of heaven. Believers who intend to live there should become familiar with their future home.

I. **The Dimensions of the City**

II. **The Description of the City**
   A. The Holy City
   B. The Pearly Gates
   C. The Foundations of Precious Stones
   D The Streets of Gold
   E. The Lamb That Is the Light
   F. The Tree of Life
   G. The River of Life

III. **The Denial to the City**

OVERVIEW

My wife and I have had the privilege of traveling to many of the world's most beautiful cities. After growing up in a small village in Ohio called Cedarville, I went away to seminary in Dallas, Texas, and became a confirmed big-city person.

There are a lot of big cities in the United States. Juneau, Alaska, is the largest geographically (3,081 square miles—larger than Delaware!), and Jacksonville, Florida is the largest geographically in the lower forty-eight states (800 square miles). New York City, of course, is the largest in terms of population in the United States, but there are ten cities in the world that have larger populations than New York. In terms of greater metropolitan areas, Tokyo has twenty-eight million people, New York City has twenty-one million, and Mexico City has eighteen million.

To put all that in perspective, the largest city in A.D. 100 was Rome with a population of only 400,000. Today there are 100 cities in China with more than a million people, forty-five in the Americas, thirty-six in Europe, and nineteen in Africa. By the year 2030, more than 60 percent of the world's inhabitants will be living in cities.

As great as the cities of our world are, they cannot compare with the city God is building for His children to inhabit for eternity. This city is mentioned almost a dozen times in Revelation 21–22, and not metaphorically—it is an actual physical city where God and His people will live together forever. This city has been mentioned numerous times throughout Scripture as the eventual destination of man's pilgrimage (Hebrews 11:10; 12:22; Galatians 4:26; Revelation 3:12). Not surprisingly, this city is called the New Jerusalem.

The New Jerusalem is not synonymous with heaven. Rather, it is a city that is in heaven. The apostle John said he saw the New Jerusalem coming down *out of heaven* (Revelation 21:2, italics added). We can assume from Scripture that God is preparing the New Jerusalem in heaven to become the capital, so to speak, of heaven in the future. Jesus called the New Jerusalem "the city of My God" (Revelation 3:12). This is the city Jesus referred to in John 14:3 when He told His disciples He was going to prepare a place for them. During the Millennium, the thousand-year reign of Christ on earth, the New Jerusalem will hover over the earth. Then, after the Millennium, in the eternal state, it will rest on the renovated earth and serve as the focal point of life in eternity.

Its dimensions and description certainly qualify it to be a focal point!

THE DIMENSIONS OF THE CITY (21:15-16)

People often wonder how all the believers from history are going to fit into heaven and, specifically, the New Jerusalem. The basic dimensions of the city are given in Revelation 21:15–16. It is actually a cube 1,400 miles in length, height, and breadth. That means it covers more than 2,000,000 square miles of land area. That makes the city, in terms of land area, twenty times larger than New Zealand, ten times larger than Germany, ten times larger than France, and forty times larger than England. It is even larger than India.[1]

J. B. Smith has compared the New Jerusalem to the United States this way: "If you compare the New Jerusalem to the United States, you would measure from the Atlantic Ocean coastal line and westward, it would mean a city from the furthest Maine to the furthest Florida, and from the shore of the Atlantic to Colorado. And from the United States' Pacific coast eastward, it would cover the United States as far as the Mississippi River, with the line extending north through Chicago and continuing on the west coast of Lake Michigan, up to the Canadian border."[2]

A single city that large—and remember, it is a cube, so it extends upward as far as it does outward—is literally difficult to comprehend. But the same God who spoke the planets into existence will have no trouble building and deploying a city that large onto planet earth. Because the city is a cube, it must have "floors" inside it that extend upwards. Someone has calculated that there could be room for as many as 600 floors within the cube. If each of those 600 floors covers the same 2,000,000-plus square miles as the bottom floor, that produces 1.2 billion square miles of "living area" within the cube. (If you're wondering about transportation inside such a structure, remember that our glorified bodies will be different, that the Lord Jesus simply appeared in a room with the disciples after His resurrection, unhindered by physical barriers.)

The cubic design of the New Jerusalem should come as no surprise—the Holy of Holies inside the temple in Jerusalem was a cube: 20×20×20 cubits. And Revelation 21:3 refers to the New Jerusalem as the "tabernacle of God." So just as God's dwelling place on earth was a cube, so will the New Jerusalem, His eternal "tabernacle," be a cube as well.

THE DESCRIPTION OF THE CITY
(REVELATION 21:19–20)

In reading the following seven descriptions of the New Jerusalem, be aware that many people allegorize, or spiritualize, these elements of the city. They simply can't imagine that anything like what John describes in Revelation could possibly exist one day. I choose to submit my human reason and understanding to the Word of God and view these descriptions literally. I can't imagine how God could have created the heavens and the earth either, but I choose to believe that He did. Likewise I choose to believe the amazing descriptions of the New Jerusalem we are given in Scripture.

The Holy City (Revelation 21:2)

First, we read that the New Jerusalem is a "holy city." I've seen some big cities in the world, but I've never seen a holy one. Here's how the *Wycliffe Bible Commentary* describes the holy city: "A holy city will be one in which no lie will be uttered in one hundred million years, no evil word will ever be spoken. No shady business deals will ever be discussed, no unclean picture will ever be seen, no corruption of life will ever be manifest. It will be holy because everyone in it will be holy." [3]

Only those who have been cleansed of their sins by the blood of Christ will be able to enter the holy city.

The Pearly Gates (21:12, 17, 18, 21)

The "pearly gates" of heaven have assumed the status of folklore, but they are real. Revelation 21:21 says, "The twelve gates were twelve pearls: each individual gate was of one pearl." The gates have the names of the 12 tribes of Israel on them, and are part of a city that glimmers and shines like a sparkling jewel, given the gold and precious jewels of which it is made.

W. A. Criswell has pointed out that pearls are formed in oysters as a result of a wound, and that we'll be reminded as we go in and out of the gates of pearl that we are there only because of the wounds of Christ. [4]

The Foundations of Precious Stones
(Revelation 21:19–20)

A twelve-layer foundation of the city is built from 12 precious stones: emeralds, sapphires, topaz, and the like. Looking at these layers of beautiful stones will be like looking at a shimmering rainbow with light reflecting off of and through them into the city.

The Streets of Gold (Revelation 21:18–21)

Heaven's streets of gold are also part of folklore to many, but they couldn't be more real: "The street of the city was pure gold, like transparent glass" (verse 21). Gold as we know it is not transparent. Perhaps this refers more to translucence than transparency due to the purity of the gold. It's hard to say how we will see and perceive things in our glorified bodies compared to how we perceive them today. But one way or another, what John saw was streets of transparent gold. And I believe they will look that same way to us when we see them.

The Lamb That Is the Light (Revelation 21:11, 23)

There will be no lights in the New Jerusalem: "The Lamb is its light" (verse 23). The glory of God will illuminate the entire city (Isaiah 60:19).

Imagine approaching the city from a distance—a city of gold, a twelve-layer foundation, gates of pearl, streets of gold, fully illuminated from within by the glow of the glory of God. No wonder Paul wrote, "Eye has not seen, nor ear heard, nor have entered into the heart of man the things which God has prepared for those who love Him" (1 Corinthians 2:9).

You've heard it said that some people are "so heavenly minded they're no earthly good." I believe we should all be *more* heavenly minded, not less. God has prepared an unbelievable place in which we will live for eternity, yet we rarely talk about it; and most Christians know little about it at all. We might be more earthly good if we were more heavenly minded!

The Tree of Life (Revelation 22:2)

There is a river flowing through the middle of the New Jerusalem, and on either side are growing the trees of life ("trees" is plural in the original). There are twelve trees of life "which bore twelve fruits, each tree yielding its fruit every month." These have to be the same as the tree of life in the Garden of Eden (Genesis 2:9), and we will eat from them freely—which raises the issue of eating in heaven. I believe we will eat freely, as much as we want, without any of the negative ramifications of our earthly appetites. Our appetites in heaven will be redeemed along with the rest of us, so our perspective on food will be different.

The leaves of the trees are for "the healing of the nations." "Healing" is the Greek word for therapy; so this healing is not the healing of diseases, but healing in a therapeutic sense: growing in our sense of fulfillment, pleasure, and joy at being in the presence of God.

The River of Life (Revelation 22:1–2)

The last thing we'll highlight is the "pure river of water of life, clear as crystal, proceeding from the throne of God and of the Lamb." This sounds like Psalm 46:4: "There is a river whose streams shall make glad the city of God." It also calls to mind the "living water" Jesus said would flow from the heart of those who believe in Him (John 7:38).

The New Jerusalem will be something impossible to comprehend in its glory while we are on earth. But it will be the future home of every person who has been a believer, children who have died without the chance to believe, those not mentally capable of believing the Gospel. The cube-city will be large enough to sustain all those millions of people at a level of glory and satisfaction far beyond anything ever experienced on earth. It will be beautiful and radiant—words fail us to describe its glory.

There is an island-city in Greece called Santorini that is built on the top of an ancient volcano. It sits high on a cliff and is a fascinating place to visit—all the houses and shops are painted white. When you approach Santorini from the sea, you look up and see this gleaming white city that appears to be suspended in the air above the sea. It is an amazing site! When I saw it on one occasion, I thought to myself that even such a place as beautiful as Santorini cannot compare to the beauty of the New Jerusalem. One day when we enter the Holy City of God, our mouths will fall open at the beauty that God has prepared for us as evidence of His love.

THE DENIAL TO THE CITY (21:27)

It is unfortunate, but not every person that has lived on earth will gain entrance to the heavenly city. In Revelation 21:8 we read, "But the cowardly, unbelieving, abominable, murderers, sexually immoral, sorcerers, idolaters, and all liars shall have their part in the lake which burns with fire and brimstone, which is the second death."

Verse 27 also says, "But there shall by no means enter it anything that defiles, or causes an abomination or a lie, but only those who are written in the Lamb's Book of Life."

The Bible doesn't say that you can't have ever committed any of these sins and still enter the New Jerusalem. It refers to these sins as lifestyles—those people who have practiced those sins willingly, have never repented of them and received the forgiveness of their sins through Christ. Every person who enters the New Jerusalem will be a person who has sinned, and in many cases the sins will be some of those listed above. But they will be sins that have been repented of and forgiven and that no longer characterize the life of the one who once committed them.

Our calling as Christians today is to go throughout the world as Christ's ambassadors, telling people of the place God has prepared for them and inviting them to accept Christ's invitation to come to Him to be made ready for the City of God. We get that message out every way we can: In person, in print, on television and radio, the Internet—whatever is available, we will use. After reading the glorious description of the city God has prepared for us, doesn't it break your heart to know that some may not get to enjoy it? They at least need to know of the opportunity. If they reject Christ's invitation, that is one thing. But if they die without having heard of the opportunity, that is another. And we are accountable for their failure to hear the Good News that is for them.

Don't let "pearly gates" and "streets of gold" lull you into a false security about some pie-in-the-sky place that doesn't exist. Heaven is real and so is the New Jerusalem. But it is only for those who have received the forgiveness of sins Christ offers that makes them pure enough to enter the Holy City of God. Make sure that you are one of those who has made a reservation to stay in the New Jerusalem for all eternity. If you wait until the city appears, it will be too late.

Notes:

1. F. W. Boreham, *Wisps of Wildfire* (London: Epworth Press, 1924), 202–3.

2. J. B. Smith, *A Revelation of Jesus Christ* (Scottsdale: Herald Press, 1961), 289.

3. Charles F. Pfeiffer and Everett F. Harrison (eds), *The Wycliffe Bible Commentary* (Chicago: Moody Press, 1962), 1522.

4. W. A. Criswell, *Expository Sermons on Revelation* (Grand Rapids: Zondervan Publishing House, 1969), 130.

APPLICATION

1. What did the apostle John see descending out of heaven in his vision? (Revelation 21:2)

   a. What is the meaning of the "bride" metaphor? (verse 2; see Ephesians 5:25-27)

   b. Contrast the words in Revelation 21:3 with John 1:11 and 14 in terms of God coming to dwell among men.

   c. How will the New Jerusalem be different from the old Jerusalem? (Revelation 21:4)

   d. In what sense have Christians been able to participate spiritually in the New Jerusalem while living on earth? (Compare Revelation 21:4 with 2 Corinthians 5:17.)

   e. What is one of the primary differences between the old and new Jerusalems? (Revelation 21:22)

   f. Why will there be no need for a temple? (Revelation 21:3; compare Exodus 25:8)

   g. Where is the New Jerusalem to be located? (Revelation 21:24; compare 2 Peter 3:13)

h. Who are the only people who will dwell in the New Jerusalem? (Revelation 21:27)

i. Who will not dwell there? (Revelation 21:8, 27)

2. Read Hebrews 11:8-10.

   a. What was Abraham promised by God? (verse 8)

   b. What have we been promised by God? (Colossians 3:24; 1 Peter 1:4)

   c. How did he live in the "land of promise"? (verse 9)

   d. How do we live as we await our promised inheritance? (2 Corinthians 5:7)

   e. In what did Abraham, Isaac, and Jacob live? (verse 9)

   f. In what do we live now? (2 Corinthians 5:1, 4; 2 Peter 1:13)

   g. On what permanent dwelling place was Abraham waiting? (verses 10, 16)

h. What is the permanent dwelling place to which Christians are headed? (Revelation 22:14)

i. Under what circumstances might someone's place in the New Jerusalem be removed? (Revelation 22:19)

3. In what way should the New Jerusalem be a motivation for Christians to continue faithfully on their sojourn, as it was for Abraham?

DID YOU KNOW?

The new Jerusalem seen by John in his revelation had 12 gates with 12 angels at the gates, and the names of the 12 tribes of Israel written on them (Revelation 21:12). The walls had 12 foundation stones, each of which had the name of one of the 12 "apostles of the Lamb" (Revelation 21:14). The tree of life, in the midst of the city, bore 12 crops of fruit, a new crop each month (Revelation 22:2). The number 12 appears 22 times in the book of Revelation, a continual reference to the people of God in the Old (12 tribes of Israel) and New (12 apostles) Testaments.

WORSHIP IN HEAVEN

Revelation 4:1–11

In this lesson we discover the priority of worship in heaven.

OUTLINE

While there is a proliferation of worship music today, some Christians see worship as optional. The apostle John looked through a doorway into heaven and saw that worship was a central activity. The Christian's life should be a dress rehearsal on earth for an eternity of worship in heaven.

   I. **The Context of Worship in Heaven**

  II. **The Center of Worship in Heaven**

 III. **The Chorus of Worship in Heaven**

 IV. **The Crescendo of Worship in Heaven**

  V. **The Contrast of Worship in Heaven**
    A. Worship Is Not About Us—It's About Him
    B. Worship Is Not About Here—It's About There
    C. Worship Is Not About Now—It's About Then
    D. Worship Is Not About One—It's About Many

Wheaton College, in Wheaton, Illinois, outside Chicago, was for many years the bastion of Christian higher education in America. There are many fine Christian colleges now, but Wheaton was one of the first and remains one of the best.

For many years, the president of Wheaton College was Ray Edman, a godly man and great leader. In 1967, Dr. Edman was preaching a sermon to the students in the chapel at Wheaton on the subject of worship. He told the students about having met the king of Ethiopia once, and how he had to conform to strict protocols when going into the presence of that earthly king. He told the students that when they came into the presence of the Lord, they needed to come in a manner worthy of the King of Kings to worship.

Suddenly, in the middle of his sermon on worship, Dr. Edman collapsed and entered into the presence of the Lord he loved to worship. More than one writer commented after Dr. Edman's death that he would likely have had as seamless a transition from earth to heaven as anyone could imagine. He so loved and worshiped God while on earth that entering into an environment of worship in heaven would be no shock to his system at all.

Today in worship we experience it in three parts: Praise of God, prayer to God, and preaching about God. But in heaven only one of those will remain: Praise of God. There will be no need to pray since we will be in God's presence with all our needs met. And there won't be preaching in heaven because we will have a complete grasp of the truth about God. Therefore, praise is all that will remain. And the Bible says we will spend eternity in that activity.

Our goal on earth should be like that of Dr. Edman: To prepare ourselves for a seamless transition into the worship environment of heaven by creating that kind of environment on earth. What we learn to do in our short time on earth will prepare us for an eternity in heaven.

In this lesson we will look at Revelation 4:1–11, a central passage on the worship of God in heaven.

THE CONTEXT OF WORSHIP IN HEAVEN (REVELATION 4:1)

In John's vision, he saw a door standing open, giving him a vision into heaven. Through that door he saw something no one on earth had ever seen before: worship in heaven.

John, along with Peter and James, was part of Jesus' inner circle of disciples. He was with Jesus on the Mount of Transfiguration, in the Garden of Gethsemane, at the Crucifixion, and at the Resurrection. But in addition to these high moments in his life, John had also suffered for Jesus. In fact, when he received the vision of heaven, he was on the island of Patmos in the Mediterranean where he had been exiled by the Roman emperor (Revelation 1:9). John no doubt wondered if he was going to be killed or left on Patmos to die. It was a difficult time in his life and as a disciple of Christ.

But in the midst of that difficult time, he experienced something that no one else ever had. Perhaps the vision of heaven came at a time when he was at a low point, wondering how he would survive. Suddenly a door was opened and he found himself peering through a portal into heaven itself. I simply am at a loss for words to describe what John must have thought and felt at that moment.

THE CENTER OF WORSHIP IN HEAVEN (REVELATION 4:2–3)

The key word in these two verses is the word "throne." In fact, it might be the key word in all the book of Revelation since it occurs 46 times. "Throne" in Revelation speaks of sovereignty, authority, rule, and control. It speaks of the fact that, while on earth things may appear to be out of control, there is One in heaven who is controlling all things for His purposes.

Sometimes it appears that circumstances in our life are out of control, just as they might appear to one who lives on the Earth during the Great Tribulation. But they are not. God is on His throne in heaven working out all things by His plan and for His glory.

The Bible says, "No man shall see [God], and live" (Exodus 33:20). Therefore, when John looked into heaven, he only saw the appearance of God and tried to put it into words as best he could: ". . . like a jasper and a sardius stone in appearance; and there was a rainbow around the throne, in appearance like an emerald." A jasper stone is what we know as a diamond, and the sardius is our ruby. So John saw a brilliant, multifaceted stone that sparkled in the light. Somehow, what John saw was best described in terms of brilliance, worth, beauty, and light. Who among us could have described it any better? It is hard to find words in any human language to describe the appearance of God. All John could do, and all we can do, is describe the impact of His presence, not His person. Describing God is like describing the wind—the best we can do is describe the presence or impact or appearance of the wind, not the wind itself.

The Chorus of Worship in Heaven
(Revelation 4:4, 9–11)

By looking into heaven and seeing the throne of God, John became an unwitting observer of worship in heaven. It becomes apparent from his description that, where the throne of God is, there is worship.

John sees 24 additional thrones around the central throne of God on which were seated 24 elders, representatives of the church of the living God. There were also four living creatures around the throne who continually praised God. And when the creatures praised God, the 24 elders fell from their thrones and cast their crowns before the throne of God and worshiped Him. I cannot even imagine what that must have sounded like—multiply the "Hallelujah Chorus" from Handel's *Messiah* by infinity, and maybe it would come close!

William Temple has defined praise like this, which must be what happens in heaven: "To worship is to quicken the conscience by the holiness of God, to feed the mind with the truth of God, to purge the imagination with the beauty of God, to open the heart to the love of God and to devote the will to the purpose of God."[1] This should be the goal of every worshiper on earth as we prepare to worship before the throne of God in heaven.

The Crescendo of Worship in Heaven

"Crescendo" basically means to start small and end big, usually applied to pieces of music. In the worship songs in Revelation there is an obvious crescendo that grows throughout the book. In Revelation 1:6 there is a two-fold doxology; in 4:11 there is a three-fold doxology; in 5:13 there is a four-fold doxology. Then, when you get to 7:12 there is a seven-fold doxology: "Amen! Blessing and glory and wisdom, thanksgiving and honor and power and might, be to our God forever and ever. Amen."

The worship grows as you move through the book—a crescendo of worship to the Lord. When church choirs do that—start soft and simple and end loud and complex—it's biblical!

There's another aspect of crescendo we should consider: It's as if the crescendo of worship for God escalates in accord with the timeline of God's purposes in the world. In other words, the farther along God's timeline of history we go, the greater becomes the praise and worship for Him. There has never been in the history of Christianity an emphasis on praise and worship like there is today. Christian radio stations can't play enough praise and worship music. Churches are incorporating more of it into their services. And CD's and DVD's of praise and worship are filling the store shelves. If what I'm suggesting is accurate, this crescendo of praise and worship we are experiencing is in accord with His timeline because we are getting ever closer to the "grand finale" of His purposes on earth, ultimately culminating with the praise of God in heaven.

THE CONTRAST OF WORSHIP IN HEAVEN

In C. S. Lewis's allegory *The Great Divorce*, he tells of a man who journeys to heaven and finds it to be grander in scale and more beautiful than he could have imagined. Hell, he discovers, is the opposite, a fleck of dust by comparison with heaven. In the same way, Lewis suggests our lives in this world get smaller and smaller the more we comprehend the grandeur of heaven and eternity.[2] Seeing heaven was for John like us walking up to the edge of the Grand Canyon for the first time—speechless in wonder.

John experienced smallness and largeness at the same time on Patmos. He was probably discouraged and despairing in light of his personal circumstances. But then he was given a view of the grandeur of heaven and the majesty of heavenly worship. And he was changed. When he saw that all of heaven and earth were under the authority of God in heaven, he was able to look at his exile on Patmos in a new light. Seeing our lives against the backdrop of heaven is the best way to keep things in perspective.

By necessity, our lives are focused continually on the present— the things of this world. We face demands on our lives that require us to focus on the here-and-now. Yet heaven is no less real than this present world. In fact, it is even more real in an ultimate sense. This world is passing away, but heaven will last forever. When John's temporal world and circumstances were ushered into the presence of God, he was reminded that there is something bigger and more important than the day-to-day. He remembered that God is able to do above and beyond what we can ask and think or expect (Ephesians 3:20). He remembered that nothing is impossible for God (Luke 1:37).

We can be reminded of those same truths through worship. We may not see into heaven with our eyes, but we see the character of God through His Word and our songs of praise that proclaim His worthiness. We can hear Jesus remind us of the same things of which he reminded John: "John, I want you to know that things are not as they appear to be. I'm going to show you how things really are. I'm going to walk you into the throne room of heaven and show you genuine reality. Things are not out of control. Satan has not won. Evil has not triumphed. Peek through the door; get a glimpse of reality. God is on His throne, and such a sight will transform your heart and your mind forever."

Here are four things that we can learn from John's experience on the isle of Patmos.

Worship Is Not About Us — It's About Him!

This is easy to forget—God is the center of our worship. It's amazing how many people in churches never get their attention centered on God because they don't like the hymns, the music, the style of worship, the personality of the worship leader, the color of the choir robes or hymn books, and a hundred other things. As a result, they make worship all about them instead of about God.

When you go into a worship service with the conscious intent to praise and worship God for who He is and what He has done, you will have blinders on that keep you from seeing all the "stuff" you don't like. Worship isn't about those things. It's about God.

Worship Is Not About Here — It's About There

For God, worship exalts and extols His majesty. But for us, worship gets our minds off the things of this earth and onto the realities in heaven. The only way we can live our life on earth with the values and priorities of heaven is to continually focus on heaven. If all we ever see with our spiritual eyes are the carnal and worldly affairs of this life, we will struggle. But if we are continually reminded of God's character, His purposes and plans, and His love for us, then we walk through this world with a different gait. Colossians 3:1–3 reminds us to seek and set our minds on things above. We are citizens of heaven, and that is to be the focus of our eyes and ears and the desire of our heart.

Worship Is Not About Now — It's About Then

Paul writes in 2 Corinthians 4:16–18 that we are to look not "at the things which are seen, but at the things which are not seen. For the things which are seen are temporary, but the things which are not seen are eternal." Paul is encouraging the Corinthians (and us) to leverage everything going on in their lives against the promise of the future. The contrasts he draws in these verses are powerful: The outward man is perishing, but the inward man is being renewed. The affliction of today is light, but the weight of future glory is heavy. The things that are seen are temporal, but the things that are unseen are eternal. Worship is the corridor through which we exchange the things of this world—affliction, suffering, limitations—for the reality of heaven.

Worship Is Not About One — It's About Many

We live in a day when people don't believe they need to worship in church with the body of Christ. People claim they can worship in nature or on the golf course on Sunday morning. In the book of Revelation, what we see in heaven is corporate worship. Christianity is not an individual experience. Yes, we are saved individually, but immediately we are baptized into the body of Christ where we remain for eternity. I cannot encourage you enough to make sure that you learn to do on earth what you will be doing for eternity in heaven: Worship with the many that God has redeemed for Himself.

Because we don't know the day or hour when we will be promoted to heaven, I encourage you to make every day a full dress rehearsal for the worship that will characterize your eternal life.

Note:

1. Erwin Lutzer, *Pastor to Pastor* (Grand Rapids: Kregel Inc., 1998), 79.

2. C. S. Lewis, *The Great Divorce* (UK: Geoffrey Bles, 1945), n.p.

1. Read Revelation 4:8-11.

   a. Note the similarities in appearance between the four creatures John saw and the seraphim Isaiah saw in his vision of God on His throne. (Isaiah 6:2)

   b. What were the seraphim in Isaiah's vision doing with their six wings? (Isaiah 6:2)

   c. What reasons can you suggest for the seraphs covering their faces and feet? Of what might these acts be symbols?

   d. Why do you think the creatures in John's vision had so many eyes? (Revelation 4:8)

   e. What is the significance of their continual (day and night) praise to God? (verse 8)

   f. How do their words provide continuity with the seraphim in Isaiah's vision? (Isaiah 6:3; Revelation 4:8)

g. What significance do you find in the seraphim calling to one another instead of directing their praise directly to God? (Isaiah 6:3)

h. What practical example do you find in this? What value is there in confessing our beliefs about the character of God to one another?

i. Is the earth "full of His glory" at present, or are these prophetic words of the seraphim? (Isaiah 6:3) What value do you see in confessing that which you know the future holds even though it has not yet appeared?

j. Compare the last line of Revelation 4:8 with Exodus 3:14. How is "was and is and is to come" another way of saying "I am"?

k. How is this confession in Revelation 4:8 a statement about the sovereignty of God in all of human history? Is there any time in which He is not "Almighty"?

l. Write out a statement of your own, giving God "glory and honor and thanks." (Revelation 4:9)

m. What is one reason for giving God "glory and honor and power"? (Revelation 4:11)

n. Does that say anything to you about your stewardship of what God has created? (Genesis 1:28)

2. In heaven there is continual praise while on earth there is not. Are you prepared for that transition? Do you look forward to it? Explain.

DID YOU KNOW?

The creatures seen by Isaiah are called seraphim by the prophet (Isaiah 6:2; "seraph" is singular, "seraphim" is plural, "im" being the plural ending in Hebrew). Isaiah's vision is the only place in Scripture where heavenly creatures are called seraphim. The Hebrew root srp, from which seraph likely comes, means to burn. It also is the basis for the word for serpent as in the bronze serpent Moses mounted on a pole in Numbers 21:8-9 to save Israel from the bites of the "fiery [srp] serpents" among them (Numbers 21:6). Were the seraphim in Isaiah's vision serpentine-shaped creatures? Images of winged serpents have been uncovered by archaeologists from the Old Testament era, but it is impossible to tell if Isaiah's seraphim had that shape.

THE NEW HEAVEN AND NEW EARTH

2 Peter 3:10–13;
Revelation 21:1, 5; 22:3

In this lesson we learn that planet earth
is our eternal home.

OUTLINE

There has been much confusion about the fate of planet earth. Some have read the Bible's words about fire and burning to mean that the earth will be obliterated at the end of the age. Not so. There will be fire, but it will be restorative instead of destructive. The earth is our home forever.

I. **The Promise of a New Heaven and a New Earth**

II. **The Purification of the New Heaven and New Earth**
   A. The Information
   B. The Interpretation
   C. The Illustration

III. **The Principles of the New Heaven and New Earth**
   A. The Removal of the Sea
   B. The Reversal of the Curse
   C. The Restoration of All Things
      1. A New Appreciation for the World in Which We Now Live
      2. A New Anticipation of the World to Which We Are Going

History is filled with man's efforts to establish some kind of heaven on earth. It even shows up in the efforts of politicians when they make promises to make things better, or different, to right the wrongs of the past and create an environment where man can reach his true potential. President Roosevelt offered "The New Deal" and President Johnson proposed "The Great Society." Intellectuals like Leo Tolstoy in Russia and Henry David Thoreau in New England made efforts to create utopian living conditions. Even Lenin's Communism was an effort to create a workers' paradise where greed would be outlawed and all would prosper equally.

Of course, none of these efforts achieved what their proponents envisioned. But it was not because they longed for something unattainable. In the heart of every person is a longing for something perfect based on the eternity that God has put in every human heart (Ecclesiastes 3:11). Indeed, the idea is a godly one—and it takes God to achieve it. That is exactly why the God-Man, Jesus Christ, taught His disciples to pray, "Your kingdom come. Your will be done on earth as it is in heaven."

This prayer will be answered, but not during earth's current economy. There's no way, when sin and death are rampant on earth, that utopia will be achieved. But the hope for a "golden age" is legitimate and in the heart of every human being. Indeed, it is that hope that allowed many saints of old to endure suffering in their lives while on earth (Hebrews 11:14–16).

The human race is homesick for the Garden of Eden. In this lesson, we will look at the Scriptures that point to the new heaven and new earth that God will one day bring to pass.

THE PROMISE OF A NEW HEAVEN AND A NEW EARTH

The prophets of the Old Testament saw a new heaven and new earth coming that would last forever, one so wonderful that the former earth would not even be remembered (Isaiah 66:22; 65:17). The apostle Peter also wrote, "We . . . look for new heavens and a new earth in which righteousness dwells" (2 Peter 3:13).

The writer to the Hebrews quotes Psalm 102 which talks about the heavens and the earth perishing and growing old. Then he writes, "Like a cloak You will fold them up, and they will be changed . . ." (Hebrews 1:10–12; Psalm 102:25–27). The writer to the Hebrews says God is going to one day take this world and, like a coat, fold it up and put it away and make everything new. And, as you might expect, John saw a new heaven and new earth in his vision on Patmos: "Now I saw a new heaven and a new earth, for the first heaven and the first earth had passed away" (Revelation 21:1, 5).

So the idea of a new heaven and a new earth, ones better than our current ones, is biblical.

THE PURIFICATION OF THE NEW HEAVEN AND NEW EARTH

Next, we must consider how the transformation takes place. How do the new heaven and earth come to be?

The Information (2 Peter 3:10, 12)

There is not room in this lesson to go into all the relevant Scriptures, but here is the basic timeline for when the new heavens and new earth will come to pass: First there will be a seven-year period of tribulation on the earth terminated by the Battle of Armageddon, and brought to an end with the return of Christ to the earth. Christ then rules over all the earth for 1,000 years (the Millennium). At the end of the Millennium, Satan leads a final rebellion that is put down by Christ, after which Satan is cast into the lake of fire. The Great White Throne judgment will then consign all who have rejected Christ to the lake of fire as well.

After all of this, the last thing that happens on this earth—or to this earth—is described by Peter: "The heavens will pass away with a great noise, and the elements will melt with fervent heat; both the earth and the works that are in it will be burned up . . . . The heavens will be dissolved, being on fire, and the elements will melt with fervent heat" (2 Peter 3:10, 12).

The Interpretation

That's the information—now, what does it all mean? Many have heard this event described as something like a nuclear conflagration—the earth dissolving in an indescribable ball of fire. Randy Alcorn has verbalized his own change of thinking on this subject, which parallels my own: ". . . for many years as a Bible student and later as a pastor, I didn't think in terms of renewal or restoration. Instead, I believed God was going to destroy the earth, abandon His original design and plan, and start over by implementing a new plan in an unearthly heaven. Only in the past fifteen years have my eyes been open to what Scripture has said all along."[1]

Peter's words about burning and fire certainly sound like, well, burning and fire. But the original Greek does not suggest that interpretation. The *New International Version* has a more accurate rendering: "the earth and everything in it will be laid bare." The idea is that of being uncovered, not destroyed; purified, not burned up. The material elements of the current earth will disintegrate and fall apart and out of what remains, God will create something new.

There are two words for "new" in the Greek language. The one Peter uses (2 Peter 3:13) is the word that means new in terms of quality, not new in terms of never existing before. That means the new earth is not something that is *brand* new, but a new version of the original. It is the original earth, but in a renovated and refreshed form. At the end of the Millennium, after all the judgments and prior to the beginning of the eternal state, all the decay and corruption of the earth is going to be taken away. All evidence of disease and destruction and depravity, insofar as it impacted the physical earth, will be eliminated; the present earth will be cleansed, purified, and made new.

Commentator William Hendriksen describes the change this way: "The first heavens and the first earth have passed away . . . . The very foundations of the earth have been subjected to purifying fire. Every stain of sin, every trace of death has been removed. Out of the great conflagration, a new universe has been born. The word used in the original implies that it was new, but not 'other.' It is a new world, but not another world. "It is the same heaven and [the same earth,] but gloriously rejuvenated . . . ." [2]

God's original declaration that the earth was "very good" (Genesis 1:31) has not been rescinded. He is not going to destroy His original creation—just make it pure once again as it was in the beginning.

Again, Randy Alcorn: "God doesn't throw away His handiwork and start from scratch—instead, He uses the same canvas to repair and make more beautiful the painting marred by the vandal. The vandal doesn't get the satisfaction of destroying his rival's masterpiece. On the contrary, God makes an even greater masterpiece out of what His enemy sought to destroy." [3]

The Illustration (2 *Peter* 3:5–7)

Fortunately, Peter gives us an illustration to help us picture the renovation that is to come upon the earth: the flood in Noah's day. The Genesis flood did not annihilate the earth. In fact, the water that covered the earth is a good picture of "cleansing." Indeed, the earth remained in order for Noah and his family to inhabit it after the flood receded. Likewise, the fire that comes upon the earth at the end of the age will not destroy the earth, but renovate it. Just as the ark protected Noah and his family, the New Jerusalem, hovering over the earth during the final renovation, will be a refuge for the people of God.

THE PRINCIPLES OF THE NEW HEAVEN AND NEW EARTH

We now look at what the new heavens and new earth are going to be like. What kind of home will a renovated earth be?

The Removal of the Sea (Revelation 21:1)

One of the most surprising things we learn from Revelation 21:1 is that there will be no more sea—the oceans are gone! Three-fourths of our present world is covered by oceans, so this will certainly be something new.

Here is the explanation by world-renowned scientist, the late Dr. Henry Morris: "There will be, in fact, no need for a sea on the new earth. The present sea is needed for a reservoir for the maintenance of the hydrologic cycle . . . . In the new earth, all men and women who live there will have their glorified bodies with no more need of water. Their resurrected bodies will be composed, like that of the Lord Jesus, of flesh and bone but apparently with no need of blood to serve as a cleanser and restorer of the body's flesh as it is at present. This, in turn, eliminates the major need for water on earth (blood is 90 percent water, and present-day human flesh is about 65 percent water)."[4]

In other words, the ecology of the new earth will be totally different from that of the present earth. We have already seen in this study that the New Jerusalem will have a fresh water river flowing from the throne of God, watering the trees of life growing on its shores. But there will be no salt-water oceans. Since salt is a preservative, and there will be no decay, no salt will be needed.

The Reversal of the Curse (Revelation 22:3)

If you recall, the curse in Genesis 3 is what created our present earth environment. When Adam and Eve disobeyed God in the Garden of Eden, it resulted in God cursing the earth. The ground was cursed, causing it to produce thistles and thorns and make it difficult to grow food. Only by the sweat of his brow would Adam and his descendants be able to eke out a living. The most important part of the curse was death: Adam and Eve and their descendants would not live forever. Death became a part of the culture of planet earth.

In the new heaven and new earth, the curse will be reversed—there will be no more death. Thorns and thistles—and tombstones—will disappear from the ground. The redemption accomplished by Christ not only delivers man from death but the earth from the effects of sin as well.

The Restoration of All Things (Ephesians 1:10)

We read Ephesians 1:10 without noticing an important point: In "the fullness of the times" God is going to "gather together in one all things in Christ, *both which are in heaven and which are on earth—* in Him" (italics added).

Today there is a great division between heaven and earth—God is in heaven and man is on earth. But God is going to bring all things together under one head: Christ. Heaven and earth will be united into one new universe, ruled by the Lord Jesus Christ. The wall that divides heaven and earth today will be torn down.

We have said previously that the New Jerusalem will be our domicile as the capital city of heaven. But the New Jerusalem will be on the renovated earth. After all, what purpose would there be at the end of the Millennium for God to renovate the earth if no one was going to live on it? Some Christians are disappointed when they find out they're going to be living on earth instead of "in heaven." But it's at this point that "heaven on earth" will finally become a reality.

This is a bit of a paradigm shift for many believers, but it can lead to two new appreciations for those who embrace it.

1. A New Appreciation for the World in Which We Now Live

   Christians have a reputation for not being very good ecologists. Our mentality of being taken off the earth and spending eternity in heaven has caused us not to give the attention this earth deserves. And that violates our commission to be good stewards of the earth (Genesis 1:26).

   But that changes when we realize that this earth is going to be our eternal home. Yes, it will be a new earth, but the same earth nonetheless. That fact should cause us to look at this earth with a new set of eyes and view it differently.

   The apostle John wrote that we should not love this world (1 John 2:15), but he didn't mean the physical world.

He meant the spiritual systems of this world, empowered by Satan. But we should love and care for this planet that God has given us as a home. The fact that it is going to be our refurbished home for eternity should give us a new appreciation for it today.

2. A New Anticipation of the World to Which We Are Going

We think the starry heavens are beautiful now—and they are! But the beauty of the heavens now is nothing compared to the beauty we will one day experience. It will be a place characterized by laughter without tears and life without death and singing without mourning and contentment without crying and pleasure without pain. And our Lord and Savior, Jesus Christ, will be there as well as our loving heavenly Father and the blessed Holy Spirit. And there will be a resplendent, brilliant, and sparkling city called the New Jerusalem that will be our heavenly home.

When I think of what awaits me in heaven—and specifically, the new heavens and the new earth—I can hardly contain my excitement.

I hope you feel the same way and that you will remember the way to get there. Jesus Christ said, "I am the way, the truth, and the life. No one comes to the Father except through me" (John 14:6). If you want to be there—and I hope you do—you can only get there through Him.

Notes:

1. Randy Alcorn, *Heaven* (Wheaton: Tyndale House Publishers, 2004), 89.

2. William Hendriksen, *More Than Conquerors* (Grand Rapids: Baker, 1982), 198.

3. Alcorn, op. cit., 100.

4. Henry Morris, *The Revelation Record* (Wheaton: Tyndale House Publishers, 1983), 436.

APPLICATION

1. Read 2 Peter 3:1-14.

   a. What is Peter's purpose in writing to the believers in his two letters? (verses 1-2)

   b. What is his first warning to them? (verse 3)

   c. What claim will end-time scoffers make? (verse 4)

   d. What is at the heart of their complaint? (They see no evidence of what?)

   e. What key events in history do they fail to remember? (verses 5-6)

   f. How are those events tied to what will happen in the future? (verse 7)

   g. What do you imagine scoffers might have said to Noah in his day as he built the ark?

   h. What are the "heavens and the earth" being reserved for at the present time? (verse 7)

i. Why is time never the issue when it comes to the fulfillment of God's plans? (verses 8-9)

j. What are we looking for as a "replacement" for the current heavens and earth? (verse 13)

k. What will happen to the earth we now live on? (verses 10, 12)

l. What will be the distinguishing characteristic of the new heavens and new earth? (verse 13b)

m. What should characterize our lives as we wait for God's refurbishing of the earth? (verse 14)

2. Why do the heavens and earth need to be renovated (made righteous; 2 Peter 3:13b) before the New Jerusalem descends to the earth? (Revelation 21:1-2)

3. Read Isaiah 65:17-25.

   a. What did Isaiah's messianic vision of the future entail? (verse 17)

   b. How does Isaiah's vision of Jerusalem correspond to what you have learned about the coming New Jerusalem in Revelation 21? (verses 18-19)

c. List the various "idyllic" signs of God's blessing on Jerusalem and the new heavens and new earth in verses 20-25.

4. What part of the new heavens and new earth do you most anticipate enjoying?

DID YOU KNOW?

The end of the age and the appearing of the new heavens and new earth will happen in the "dispensation [or administration; NASB] of the fullness of the times" (Ephesians 1:10). The word "dispensation" (or administration) translates the Greek *oikonomia*, from which we get our English word "economy." Just as modern governments put together economic plans for sustaining their nations, so God has an "economy," or plan, for the sustaining of His kingdom on planet earth. That plan calls for God to "gather together in one all things in Christ, both which are in heaven and which are on earth" (Ephesians 1:10).

WHAT ON EARTH IS THE MILLENNIUM?

Revelation 20:1–10

*In this lesson we learn about
Christ's future thousand-year rule over earth.*

OUTLINE

Imagine a TV nature show where you see a lion sneaking up on a bale of hay instead of an antelope. During the Millennium, peace will rule the earth—including the animals! Christ's kingdom will be characterized by peace, prosperity, purity, prolonged life, and personal joy.

I. **Three Perspectives on the Millennium**
   A. Post-Millennialism
   B. A-Millennialism
   C. Pre-Millennialism

II. **Four Purposes of the Millennium**
   A. To Reward the People of God
   B. To Respond to the Prophets' Predictions
   C. To Receive the Answer to the Disciples' Prayer
   D. To Reemphasize Man's Depravity and the Necessity of Christ's Death

III. **Five Profiles of the Millennium**
   A. It Will Be a Time of Peace
   B. It Will Be a Time of Prosperity
   C. It Will Be a Time of Purity
   D. It Will Be a Time of Prolonged Life
   E. It Will Be a Time of Personal Joy

OVERVIEW

Almost everyone knows the lyrics to Isaac Watts' famous hymn, "Joy to the World," but few people realize that it is not really a Christmas hymn. A quick look at the lyrics will explain why:

Joy to the world, the Lord is come!
Let earth receive her King;
Let every heart prepare Him room,
And heaven and nature sing . . . .
[Did mankind receive the king when Jesus was born at Bethlehem?]

Joy to the earth, the Savior reigns!
Let men their songs employ;
While fields and floods, rocks, hills and plains,
Repeat the sounding joy . . . .
[Has nature rejoiced at the coming of Christ?]

No more let sins and sorrows grow,
Nor thorns infest the ground;
He comes to make His blessing flow
Far as the curse is found . . . .
[Has the curse been lifted from the earth?]

He rules the world with truth and grace,
And makes the nations prove
The glories of His righteousness,
And wonders of His love . . . .
[Is Jesus ruling the nations of the world?]

The words of this great hymn more accurately describe the coming Millennium, the time when Christ will rule over the earth at His second coming, not His first. The Millennium will be a foretaste of the heavenly state that is to follow. Revelation 20:1–10 is the central passage in the Bible on the Millennium and will be our focus in this lesson.

"Millennium" is a Latin word made up of two words: *Mille* means "thousand," and *annum* means "years." Therefore, combining the two yields millennium, or a period of a thousand years. "Millennium" doesn't occur in our English Bibles, but the reference to a thousand-year period of time does—six times in Revelation 20:1–10. As we will see in this lesson, the Millennium is a period of one thousand years that begins with Christ's second coming to earth. He establishes His kingdom in Jerusalem and brings in a period of peace and justice on the earth.

Christians through the years have viewed the Millennium from three different perspectives.

THREE PERSPECTIVES ON THE MILLENNIUM

Few topics in Bible interpretation generate as much heat among Christians as does the Millennium because of the way one's view impacts other end-time events.

Post-Millennialism

The word "post," when used as a prefix, means "after." Therefore, Post-Millennialists believe that Christ's second coming will occur after the Millennium.

A Unitarian minister named Daniel Whitby originated this view in the mid-seventeenth century. This view suggests that the church will saturate the world with the Gospel. Its impact on people and culture will be radical, transforming the earth into a place of peace and prosperity where the worship of God is universal. Christ will then return to inherit the peaceable kingdom that His gospel has brought about.

Post-Millennialism was popular until World War I shattered the notion that mankind could ever bring about universal peace. Then World War II happened, further reinforcing the notion of man's sinfulness, not his goodness. This view has lost credibility ever since as universal peace has been a rare commodity despite the spread of the Gospel.

A-Millennialism

The prefix "a" on a word acts to negate the meaning of the word (amoral means without morals). Therefore, A-Millennialism means there will be no literal Millennium, no thousand year period of time. The "thousand" in Revelation 20:1–10 is purely symbolic according to this view.

Proponents of this view believe the events described in Revelation 20:1–10 are happening now; they have been working themselves out in the church over the last 2,000 years. The church is reigning with Christ at present, this view holds. The peace and prosperity assigned to the Millennium is a spiritual peace and prosperity, not a literal one.

The key to this view is to spiritualize certain parts of the Bible—assigning spiritual meaning to literal words. That is, when the Bible says "a thousand years," it doesn't really mean a thousand literal years. There is a deeper spiritual meaning that is assigned to the text. The problems with that method of interpretation are obvious.

Pre-Millennialism

The prefix "pre" obviously means "before." Pre-Millennialism teaches that the return of Jesus Christ to earth will happen before the Millennial period, not after (Post-Millennialism). Christ will defeat the enemies of God (the Battle of Armageddon) and establish a thousand-year reign of peace and justice on earth.

Here's a simple diagram showing where the Millennium fits in God's plan:

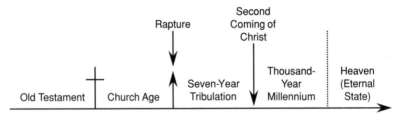

This diagram will be familiar to many as a diagram of Pre-Millennial eschatology (doctrine of the last things). After the crucifixion, Christ returns in the air to remove His church from the earth. Dead believers are resurrected and living believers follow them into the air where they meet the Lord. The seven-year Tribulation ensues, concluded by the Battle of Armageddon where Christ returns to defeat the enemies of God. The second coming of Christ inaugurates the thousand-year reign of Christ, a time of universal peace on earth. At the conclusion of the Millennium, the Great White Throne judgment consigns the wicked, the devil, and his angels to the lake of fire. The earth is renovated, the New Jerusalem descends upon the earth, and the eternal state begins.

The Pre-Millennial view holds that all the promises made to Israel in the Old Testament are fulfilled, and believing Jews are returned to their homeland in Israel to serve their Messiah, Jesus Christ.

The Pre-Millennial view is the oldest interpretation of Revelation 20:1–10 in church history and is embraced by more evangelical Christians today than any other view of the Millennium.

Four Purposes of the Millennium

There are four purposes for the thousand-year period of time on earth, each supporting the necessity for a literal thousand-year period of time on earth.

To Reward the People of God

There are many promises in the Bible about rewards that are to be given to the people of God for their faithful service (Isaiah 40:10; Matthew 16:27; 25:34; Colossians 3:24; Revelation 22:12). A kingdom has been prepared, Jesus said, for those blessed of the Father as an inheritance (Matthew 25:34); and Paul said that Christians will receive the "reward of the inheritance" (Colossians 3:24).

This reward is different from the reward of the crowns we discussed in a previous lesson. The Millennial kingdom is a reward by which we will reign and rule with Christ over the earth for a thousand years (Matthew 19:28; 1 Corinthians 6:2; Revelation 20:4). When Christ returns to earth, He will bring with Him the saints who have believed in Him. The twelve apostles will sit on twelve thrones "judging the twelve tribes of Israel" (Matthew 19:28). Our responsibilities in the Millennium will be based on our faithfulness in this life (Matthew 25:14–30).

Randy Alcorn has written these helpful words on this subject: "The idea of service as a reward is foreign to a lot of people who don't like their work, who only put up with their work until it's time to retire. We think that faithful service should be rewarded with a long vacation. But God offers us an opportunity very different from work: More responsibilities is His reward. Increased opportunities is His reward, greater abilities and resources and wisdom and empowerment. We will have sharper minds, stronger bodies, clearer purpose and unabated joy."[1]

To Respond to the Prophets' Predictions

The second purpose of the Millennium is to fulfill the words of the Old Testament prophets. Without the Millennium, the Old Testament Scriptures are left open-ended and unfulfilled. Here are just a few that are yet to be fulfilled:

- Psalm 72:11 Kings and nations must worship Christ.
- Isaiah 9:7 The Messiah's government must be established on David's throne.
- Isaiah 60:21 Israel must turn to righteousness and inherit her land forever.

- Zechariah 9:10 The nations must live in peace under Messiah's rule.
- Luke 1:32–33 Christ must rule over Israel as her Messiah in an unbroken rule.

Without the Millennium, these and many other prophecies would go unfulfilled. The focus of God's promises to Israel was that she was and is His chosen nation to be ruled over by the Prince of Peace. That has not happened yet, so it must happen in the future. Christ was rejected once by Israel (John 1:11), but He will ultimately be received by her (Zechariah 12:10). The kingdom that the apostles were looking for (Acts 1:6) will indeed come to pass for a thousand years in the Millennium.

To Receive the Answer to the Disciples' Prayer

Jesus taught His disciples to pray, "Your kingdom come. Your will be done on earth as it is in heaven" (Matthew 6:10). That prayer, prayed innumerable times through the centuries of church history, remains unanswered. With the Millennium, will come the kingdom of God on earth—and the answer to the disciples' prayer.

To Reemphasize Man's Depravity and the Necessity of Christ's Death

Satan will be bound during the Millennium (Revelation 20:2–3). But the last phrase of Revelation 20:3 says he will be released for a "little while" at the end of the thousand years, at which time he will lead a rebellion against Christ, the king (Revelation 20:7–9). People forget that during the thousand years on earth, the righteous believers who enter the kingdom will bear children—but righteousness is not inherited. The sin nature of man will still be alive and well, and some will not submit to the rule of King Jesus then any more than they do now. Though with Satan being out of the picture for a thousand years, the sin nature of man will not be enticed as it is now. But when Satan is released, he will stir up rebellion against God just as he did in the Garden of Eden.

This experience will demonstrate that sin is man's fundamental problem—not the environment, training, education, influences, or genetics. At the end of the Millennium, at the Great White Throne judgment, no one will be able to blame their environment. Even with Christ on the throne in a righteous world, some will still choose to rebel.

Five Profiles of the Millennium

Following are five characteristics of the Millennium—what life will be like during the thousand years.

It Will Be a Time of Great Peace

It will take more than the United Nations to bring "peace on earth and good will toward men." Indeed, it will take God himself. The Scriptures are full of predictions concerning the peace that one day will characterize planet earth. The famous words of Micah 4:3 are a well-known example:

> "He shall judge between many peoples,
> And rebuke strong nations afar off;
> They shall beat their swords into plowshares,
> And their spears into pruning hooks;
> Nation shall not lift up sword against nation,
> Neither shall they learn war anymore."

Isaiah 11:6–9 is another well-known passage that indicates there will be peace even in the animal kingdom and between man and the beasts of the field. There will be no armies, no military budgets, and no wars. What the United Nations has tried to do, Jesus will bring to pass.

It Will Be a Time of Prosperity

Everyone is seeking prosperity in this world, but the Millennium will be a time of prosperity like nothing ever seen before. Most of the promises given to Israel concerning future prosperity were given in agricultural terms because that was common in that day. But the same environment that will allow agriculture to abound will also support prosperity in other endeavors as well.

Consider the words of Ezekiel 34:26–27 as an example.

> "I will make them and the places all around My hill a blessing; and I will cause showers to come down in their season; there shall be showers of blessing. Then the trees of the field shall yield their fruit, and the earth shall yield her increase. They shall be safe in their land; and they shall know that I am the Lord, when I have broken the bands of their yoke and delivered them from the hand of those who enslaved them."

Amos 9:13 says, "The plowman shall overtake the reaper," and Isaiah 35:1 says, "The desert shall rejoice and blossom as the rose."

Prosperity will cover the earth like the morning dew.

It Will Be a Time of Purity

Sin will be kept in check, and disobedience will be dealt with efficiently. Christ's rule will be righteous and His kingdom will be holy.

Isaiah 11:9 says, "The earth shall be full of the knowledge of the Lord as the waters cover the sea." And Zechariah 13:2 says, "I will cut off the names of the idols from the land, and they shall no longer be remembered. I will also cause the prophets and the unclean spirit to depart from the land."

An amazing thing will happen during the Millennium: "In those days ten men from every language of the nations shall grasp the sleeve of a Jewish man, saying, 'Let us go with you, for we have heard that God is with you'" (Zechariah 8:23). Christ's presence will be known and felt all over the earth, and many will willingly respond to His rule in submission.

It Will Be a Time of Prolonged Life

We know that life spans were hundreds of years long before the Genesis flood and declined steadily thereafter. But in the Millennium, people will once again live long lives. In fact, a hundred-year-old person will be considered to be still a child (Isaiah 65:20). If a person 100 years old is viewed as a child, then it appears life spans will revert to pre-flood lengths: seven, eight, and nine hundred years long. Science has failed to produce a "Fountain of Youth," but the Millennium will restore longevity to all inhabitants of planet earth.

It Will Be a Time of Personal Joy

Because of the rule of a righteous King whose justice will keep life in balance around the world, many of the causes of heartache will be removed. The Millennium will be a time of unprecedented joy as a natural by-product of peace. Isaiah 14:7 says, "The whole earth is at rest and quiet; they break forth into singing." When was the last time you heard people at a shopping mall break forth into singing because of their joy?

The day is coming, as Paul wrote, when every knee will bow and every tongue will confess that Christ is Lord (Philippians 2:10–11)—and it is called the Millennium. If you want to live to see that day, you must begin today by bowing and confessing that Jesus is Lord.

Note:

1. Randy Alcorn, *Heaven* (Wheaton: Tyndale House Publishers, 2004), 226.

1. Read Isaiah 9:7.

   a. From whose throne would the coming Messiah rule over His kingdom?

   b. Of what would there be no end in His kingdom?

   c. By what two standards would the Messiah's kingdom be ordered and established?

   d. When would the kingdom end once Messiah took the throne?

   e. Identify several traits of the Millennial kingdom of Christ that are consistent with Isaiah's vision? (Revelation 20:1-10).

2. Read Isaiah 11:1-10.

   a. What will characterize the rule of the "Rod from the stem of Jesse as He rules and judges? (verse 2)

   b. What will He use as His benchmark for ruling—and what will He not use? (verses 3-4)

c. Why is righteousness the defining trait that characterizes God's judgments and rule? (verses 4-5)

d. What imagery does verse 5 call to mind? (See Ephesians 6:13-17)

e. When the Rod of Jesse rules on earth, how will it affect the natural world? (verses 6-8)

f. What will be missing from the earth? (verse 9a)

g. Of what will the earth be full? (verse 9b)

h. How will the nations of the earth respond to the "Root of Jesse" and His rule? (verse 10)

i. Who is this descendant of Jesse? (Matthew 1:6, 16; Luke 3:23, 31)

j. How did the prophet Amos see the restoration of David's throne in the future? (Amos 9:11-12; Acts 15:16-18)

k. What connection do you see in Paul's efforts on behalf of the Gentiles in Acts 15:19 and the prophet's anticipation of Gentiles entering the future kingdom of God? (Isaiah 11:10; Amos 9:12)

3. What was the central message of John the Baptist and Jesus of Nazareth at the beginning of their ministries? (Matthew 3:2; 4:17, 23; 5:3, 10, 19-20).

a. What did Jesus teach His disciples to pray for? (Matthew 6:10)

b. What aspect of the millennial kingdom of Christ do you most anticipate in terms of its reversal of current conditions on earth?

DID YOU KNOW?

The English word "millennium" is derived from two Latin words: *mille* (thousand) and *annum* (year). Within the Christian tradition, three schools of interpretation have developed about the Millennium, or thousand-year rule of Christ mentioned in Revelation 20:1-6. Premillennialists take this reign literally, the "pre" referring to Christ's return being before the Millennium as taught in this study guide. Amillennialists believe the thousand years should be taken figuratively, not literally; that it refers to the present period in which Christ's victorious rule over Satan and death is experienced. And postmillennialists believe the church creates a righteous reign on earth for a thousand years, following which Christ returns.

WHAT ABOUT THE CHILDREN?

Selected Scriptures

In this lesson we learn what happens to children who die before the age of accountability.

OUTLINE

There is no grief as deep as that of a parent who loses a child—at any age. But when a child dies as an infant or at a young age, how does God view their eternal destiny? The Bible gives assurance to all parents who lose a child prior to the child being able to place faith in Christ.

  I. **The Character of God**

 II. **The Condition for Salvation**

III. **The Compassion of the Savior**

IV. **The Child of David**

 V. **Conclusion**
   A. What About the Age of Accountability?
   B. How Old Will Children Be in Heaven?

After seminary my first pastoral duties were in a large church in Haddon Heights, New Jersey, where I served as Youth Pastor and Christian Education Director. Not long after my wife and I arrived at the church, the senior pastor took a few days of vacation and left me in charge of almost everything. This was a pretty scary assignment for someone fresh out of seminary, but I didn't realize exactly how scary it was about to get.

During those days when the pastor was gone, his secretary called me and asked me to pay a visit to a young couple in the church. They had lost their infant daughter to crib death—the baby had died mysteriously in its sleep. My job was to comfort and encourage them in their hour of grief, and the heart of this lesson is what I shared with them that day.

I can't think of anything more agonizing than the death of a child. Someone has said that the death of a child is like putting a period before the sentence is even finished.[1] If the loss of a child isn't grievous enough, then comes the question of that child's eternal destiny. In this lesson we will look at four reasons for believing that all infants and small children who die go straight to heaven.

THE CHARACTER OF GOD

The first reason is the character of God himself, not the least of which is the fact that He is called "Father" in the Bible (Romans 8:15). That is an initial clue as to how He regards the helpless and innocent among us.

God is compassionate, gracious, longsuffering and abundant in mercy and truth (Psalm 86:15). He is also "good to all, and His tender mercies are over all His works" (Psalm 145:9). These traits of God tell us He would never judge anyone unjustly, such as children who don't have the ability to understand the Gospel. Some say this should also exclude adults who have not heard the Gospel, but Romans 1 and Psalm 19 tell us that the evidence of God in nature surrounds us and holds all men accountable. But babies are different—they cannot understand language, reason, or the evidence in nature.

Interestingly, when the people of Israel were held accountable for not trusting God to give them victory going into the Promised Land, their children were not: "Moreover your little ones and your children . . . who today have no knowledge of good and evil, they shall go in there; to them I will give it, and they shall possess it" (Deuteronomy 1:39). The adults were penalized for their unbelief, but the children were not.

Another example is the 120,000 children of Nineveh (Jonah 4:11). Though the Ninevites were a cruel people, deserving of judgment, God had mercy on the city because of the large number of children "who [could not] discern between their right hand and their left." God's justice accounts for those not able to believe.

In Ezekiel 16:20, God refers to children as His, and in Jeremiah 2:34 and 19:4 refers to them as "innocents." Yes, children are born into sin just like everyone else, but their sins are not willful and premeditated. Thus He calls them "innocents."

God is compassionate and merciful and does not judge children who lack the ability themselves to judge.

THE CONDITION FOR SALVATION

Small children don't have the ability to understand that an affirmative response to the Gospel is the condition for salvation. They don't know what they must do to be saved (Acts 16:30–31).

Galatians 5:19–21 gives a long list of the behaviors of those who are in rebellion against God; and Revelation 21:8 has a similar, but shorter list. The point is that you cannot go to heaven if you choose to live this way; you cannot go to heaven in your sin. As Ezekiel 18:20 says, "The soul who sins shall die. . . . And the wickedness of the wicked shall be upon himself." The problem is, children don't understand this.

John MacArthur has written, "Little children have no record of unbelief or evil works, and therefore there is no basis for their deserving an eternity apart from God . . . . They are graciously and sovereignly saved by God as part of the atoning work of Jesus Christ." [2]

Before a child knows how to choose between good and evil, he or she is protected from judgment for sin by the blood of the Lord. If one cannot reasonably accept or reject the payment for sin made by Christ, that person is accepted by God. "In the Bible, infants, little children and others who cannot believe are neither told to believe or expected to do so." [3]

Since the condition for salvation is accepting the Gospel, the inability to do so spares one the judgment for not having done so.

THE COMPASSION OF THE SAVIOR

Jesus' love for little children is seen on more than one occasion in the Gospels. Indeed, the references to Jesus' interaction with children also include the adjective "little," as if to highlight His tender compassion toward little ones (Matthew 19:13–14; Mark 10:13–14). In Luke 18:15–17 the reference is to infants, or little babies, who are brought to Him.

Perhaps the most meaningful reference is Matthew 18:14 where Jesus says, "Even so it is not the will of your Father who is in heaven that one of these little ones should perish." It could not be more clear from this verse that Jesus is not willing for little ones (Greek *micros*, from which our word "micro" derives) to be lost.

What about children lost through miscarriage or abortions? My wife and I lost our first child five months into the pregnancy by miscarriage, and it was heartbreaking. I believe that this child of ours we've never met has been in heaven for decades and that we'll be united with him or her when we get there. Of our five children, one is already in heaven. I believe the Bible is clear that life and personhood begin at conception. Therefore, any persons conceived but not born are persons nonetheless and are taken to heaven when they die from miscarriage or abortion. All women who have suffered either of these experiences should expect to be reunited with these precious ones in heaven. The same is true for children who, due to mental impairment, never develop fully to the point that they can understand and receive the Gospel.

THE CHILD OF DAVID

In 2 Samuel 12, we find the story of the child of King David that provides compelling evidence for the salvation of children. You may remember David's story—he committed adultery with Bathsheba who became pregnant with David's child. After the child was born, God sent the prophet Nathan to confront David over his sin of adultery and of having Bathsheba's husband, Uriah, killed.

As part of God's judgment upon David, Nathan told him that the child born to Bathsheba would be taken away in death. The child became ill and for a week David fasted and prayed for the child to live. But on the seventh day it died. David then arose, washed and anointed himself and went into the temple to worship the Lord. He then asked for something to eat. His servants were confused. They couldn't understand why David was not fasting and mourning after the child died instead of before. David's reply was, "Now he is dead; why should I fast? Can I bring him back again? I shall go to him, but he shall not return to me" (verse 23).

In other words, David was confident that he would see his child again. David believed he was going to heaven when he died, and that is where he expected to see his son. Even though the idea of heaven was not as fully understood theologically in the Old Testament as in the New Testament, David still believed that he and his son would be reunited in the place of God's blessing where believers went after death.

David understood then what we now know to be true: Small children and infants go to be with the Lord when they die.

CONCLUSION

There are legitimate questions to be raised, and we'll deal with two of them here: The age of accountability and the age of children in heaven.

What About the Age of Accountability?

People are always looking for a specific age by which to define the age of accountability. But the age at which a child becomes accountable for the message of the Gospel is as different as are children themselves. No two children develop at the same rate and in the same way. They all are on different developmental paths. Children are sinners from the moment of their conception. But they are covered by the blood of Christ that "takes away the sin of the world" (John 1:29) until they can understand their sin and resulting guilt before God. Isaiah 7:16 makes reference to a child (actually, the coming Messiah) and his ability "to refuse the evil and choose the good"—so there is a time when a child crosses that line. But the Bible does not give an age at which that happens.

Parents need to be sensitive to their children to discern when their understanding has developed sufficiently to be accountable for what they are learning about Christ, sin, and the Gospel. If children are raised in a Christian home, conversations will happen that let parents know how their children are developing spiritually. Growing up in a pastor's home, I would see people get saved and be baptized in church when I was small, and I would ask my father questions about those experiences at home. Children may commit themselves to Christ at an early age, and do it several more times as they mature. I was actually baptized twice, once after professing my faith as a child and then again as a young adult when I felt I fully understood the implications of the Gospel.

The "moment of accountability" will happen as a child begins to express understanding after hearing a Sunday school lesson or after a conversation with a parent. Each of my four children came to know Christ at different times and in different ways, as I'm sure is true for most parents with their children. The main challenge is for parents to be sensitive. When we have child dedication services in our church, we are really dedicating the parents to the task of staying sensitive to their children and leading them to Christ as soon as they are able to understand their need for the Gospel.

Many parents also wonder about the age for baptism. Children should only be baptized when they can understand and explain the Gospel themselves, when they can express assurance of their own salvation. And the same should be true for participating in the Lord's Table.

Parents should not be anxious about children who go to be with the Lord. God is just and compassionate and receives little ones to himself with open arms. Nor should they be anxious about the age of accountability. Prayer and sensitivity to the Lord's leading will allow you to minister the Gospel to your child at the appropriate time. The main thing is to make sure you are a Christian yourself. You cannot impart what you do not possess.

How Old Will Children Be in Heaven?

Finally, we consider the question of children's ages in heaven. That is, when a child dies, especially as an infant (and certainly those who never reach full term and are born), will that child be a child in heaven or a mature adult. If an infant dies at too young an age to understand God on earth, how could that child enjoy and appreciate God in heaven as an infant? Some argue that the book of Revelation depicts *everyone* in heaven worshipping God, which suggests that all will be able to do that in terms of age and maturity— that is, as adults.

Alister McGrath suggests this interesting perspective: "As each person reaches their peak of perfection around the age of thirty, they will be resurrected as they would have appeared at that time— even if they had never lived to reach that age . . . The New Jerusalem will thus be populated with men and women as they would appear at the age of 30 . . . but with every blemish removed."[4]

We know from Isaiah 11:8 that there will be infants and children in the Millennium: "The nursing child shall play by the cobra's hole, and the weaned child shall put his hand in the viper's den." So, if the millennium is part of heaven, there's some reason to believe that perhaps children will be in heaven and allowed to grow until they reach maturity at around the age of thirty—then sort of "frozen" in time. (Many of us would love to be frozen in time at around that age, I suspect!)

Another perspective is that of J. Vernon McGee: "I believe with all my heart that God will raise the little ones such that the mother's arms who have ached for them will have the opportunity of holding them. The father's hand which never held the little hand will be given the privilege. I believe that little ones will grow up in the care of their earthly parents, if they are saved."[5]

To summarize, we certainly do not know with certainty about the age of children in heaven. The Bible simply does not say. Whatever God's answer to this question is, we know it will be a wholly satisfying one to parents who have lost small children whom God has taken to heaven.

A family once lost their infant child. When an older sister asked where her new little baby brother was, the mother said, "He's gone to be with Jesus." Later, the older child heard her mother expressing her grief to a friend over having lost her baby. The little girl asked her mother, "Is something lost when you know where it is?" "No, dear, " the mother replied. "Then how can our baby be lost when we know he's with Jesus?" the wise little girl asked.

A baby is not lost when you know where it is, and babies who die at an early age are with Jesus.

Notes:

1. http://www.backtothebible.org/bigquestions/bq_bigquestions.htm

2. John MacArthur, *Safe in the Arms of God* (Nashville: Thomas Nelson Publishers, 2003), 81.

3. Robert Lightner, *Safe in the Arms of Jesus* (Grand Rapids: Kregel, 2000), 15–16, 25.

4. Randy Alcorn, *Heaven* (Wheaton: Tyndale House Publishers, 2004), 289.

5. Quoted by Woodrow Kroll, *Is My Child in Heaven?* (Lincoln: Back to the Bible, 1996).

1. From these verses, note all the attributes of God that are mentioned:

   a. Psalm 86:15

   b. Exodus 33:19

   c. Exodus 34:6-7

   d. Numbers 14:18

   e. Nehemiah 9:17

   f. Psalm 86:15

   g. Psalm 103:8

   h. Psalm 145:8

   i. Joel 2:13

   j. Jonah 4:2

   k. How do these attributes of God influence your consideration of how God treats the innocent among us?

l. If you are a parent, how often do you find yourself responding with these same attributes toward your own children?

m. What factors help you know whether your children are "responsible" or "not responsible" for their actions?

n. Even when your child knows better, what prompts you at times to forgive him or her anyway?

o. How did God display His attributes of compassion and forgiveness with David, king of Israel? (2 Samuel 11-12, especially verse 12:13)

2. Read Luke 12:47-48.

a. What is the difference between the two punishments meted out by the master?

b. What does this parable of Jesus suggest about God's "fairness" or "justice" in dealing with humanity?

c. How much responsibility is "given" to children? Therefore, how much obedience is "required"? (verse 48)

d. How does this parable on "proportionality" inform your understanding of God's dealings with children?

3. Read Matthew 19:13.

   a. What does this vignette reveal about the differences in how God and man view children?

   b. What do you think His welcoming attitude reveals that could be applied to the question of the eternal destiny of children?

   c. When anyone—child or adult—moves toward God (toward Jesus, in this case), what is God's response?

   d. What do you find inconsistent with God's character in the idea of innocent children not being welcomed in heaven?

DID YOU KNOW?

The Greek language used a variety of words to describe children in light of a number of variables: age, maturity, and relationship to others. A *teknon* was a child, a *teknion* was a little child, a *huios* was a son, a *pais* was a child in relation to order in the family, age, or condition, a *paidion* was a "little" *pais,* and a *paidarion* referred to boys and girls. In addition, *nerios* meant childish, *monogenes* meant an only (begotten) child, and *teknogonia* referred to bearing children. The apostle John was fond of referring to Christians as children—either his spiritual children or children of God—the word occurring 18 times in his three epistles. (W. E. Vine, *Vines Complete Expository Dictionary,* under the word "child.")

TOUGH-MINDED ABOUT HEAVEN

2 Peter 3:10–18

In this lesson we learn what it means to discipline ourselves to stay focused on heaven.

OUTLINE

It's often said, "Out of sight, out of mind." And that's what happens to some believers regarding heaven. Because we can't see it, we become lax in our preparation for it. But heaven is real, Christ is coming, and we must exercise ourselves to be ready for that Day.

I. **Tough-Minded About Our Purity**

II. **Tough-Minded About His Promises**

III. **Tough-Minded About Our Purpose**

IV. **Tough-Minded About Our Profession**

V. **Tough-Minded About Our Progress**
   A. Growth Comes Through the Will of God
   B. Growth Comes Through the Watchfulness of Prayer
   C. Growth Comes Through the Word of God
   D. Growth Comes Through the Work of the Church

When I deliver a biblical message about heaven, I have Christians ask me, "Pastor, should we be spending so much time thinking about heaven? Shouldn't we be focusing our energies on the important issues we face here on earth? After all, we'll have all of eternity to learn about heaven." Or, in the words of author Wayne Martindale, "If you're thinking about the heavenly streets of gold, aren't you likely to forget about the potholes in the streets of Chicago?" [1]

If we didn't have the New Testament, that might be a reasonable question. But one of the central thoughts of Scripture is, what we think about heaven has a great deal to do with how we live on earth. Heaven is like an anchor to which we are tied, and it is pulling us through the present into the future.

In his second epistle, Peter summarizes this thought with a piercing question. He has just described how the earth is going to be renovated by fire at the end of the age, and asks, "Therefore, since all these things will be dissolved, what manner of persons ought you to be . . . ?" (2 Peter 3:11) That is, in light of God's plan for eternity, how should you be living your life in the present? He then proceeds to answer his own question, and that is our focus in this final lesson in our series of studies on heaven.

Hopefully, you now know a great deal more about heaven than when you began this study. And knowledge leads to responsibility and accountability. You and I should be different people today in light of what we have learned about the future.

In his first epistle, Peter encouraged his readers (and us) to "gird up the loins of [their] mind" and to "be sober" (1:13). Or, as *The Message* puts it, "Roll up your sleeves, put your mind in gear." This is a military term, meaning to pull up the folds of one's robe and tuck them in the belt so as not to impede one's forward progress. Applied to the mind, Peter is saying, "Don't be sloppy in your thinking. Don't be casual. We're in a battle and have to prepare ourselves for victory."

If we, as Christians, don't gird up our minds, we will absorb the thinking of this world. We'll start believing that the world system is all there is—that there is no future, no heaven, no rewards, no eternal worship of God, and no service of God in the new heavens and new earth. If we don't stay focused on heaven, allowing that hope to pull us purposefully through this world, we will get bogged down spiritually and lose our edge.

There are five ways we need to remain tough-minded in light of heaven, in light of the any-moment return of Jesus Christ for His church.

TOUGH-MINDED ABOUT OUR PURITY (2 PETER 3:11)

Peter asks, "What manner of persons ought you to be in holy conduct and godliness . . . ?" The Greek word *hagios* (holy) literally means "set apart." And specifically, set apart for God's service. In 1 Peter 1, where Peter urges us to be tough-minded, he goes on to say, "As He who called you is holy, you also be holy in all your conduct, because it is written, 'Be holy, for I am holy'" (verses 15–16).

In addition to being holy, Peter says we are to be godly. He echoes the words of the apostle Paul who wrote to Timothy, "Exercise yourself toward godliness. For . . . godliness is profitable for all things . . ." (1 Timothy 4:7–8). He means that godliness, like physical fitness, does not just happen—you have to work at it.

Since winning my own bout with cancer, I have been getting up and going to the gym every morning to exercise before work in order to stay healthy. Would I rather sleep in? Yes. Would I rather stay healthy than sleep in? Definitely. So I go to the gym and work out. It's the same with godliness. We have to work at it to achieve the end result.

What are the exercises? Bible study, prayer, self-control, discipline in what we watch, read, and listen to, accountability, fellowship, worship, service, and giving. In order to be godly, those are the exercises we must carry out.

The opposite of pursuing godliness is denying ungodliness. In Titus 2:12 Paul wrote, "Denying ungodliness and worldly lusts, we should live soberly, righteously, and godly in the present age." Pursuing godliness and denying ungodliness are not theoretical ideas, they are actionable ideas—hands-on goals to pursue. In the world we live in, anyone who is not "pursuing" and "denying" is going to get caught up in the things of this world.

The connection between the pursuit of godliness and the return of Christ is everywhere in the New Testament. Not to see the value of the study of heaven is to miss a central theme of Scripture. Here are some representative Scriptures and their central ideas:

- 1 Corinthians 1:7–8 Being blameless (holy) when Christ returns.
- Colossians 3:4–5 Put to death unholy practices in light of Christ's return.
- 1 Thessalonians 3:12–13 Having blameless (holy) hearts when Christ returns.
- 1 Thessalonians 5:23 Being blameless (sanctified) when Christ returns.
- 1 John 2:28 Not being ashamed at the time of His coming.
- 1 John 3:2–3 Purifying ourselves in light of Christ's appearing.

Whenever we contemplate the return of the perfect Son of God, it should cause us to want to be perfect as well.

Randy Alcorn, in his book on heaven (which I highly recommend), says this: "If my wedding date is on the calendar and I'm thinking of the person that I'm going to marry, I shouldn't be an easy target for seduction. Likewise, when I've meditated on heaven, sin is terribly unappealing. It's when my mind drifts from heaven that sin seems attractive. Thinking of heaven leads, inevitably, to pursuing holiness. Our high tolerance for sin testifies of our failure to prepare for heaven. If I believe I'll spend eternity in a world of unending beauty and adventure, will I be content to spend all of my evenings staring at game shows, sitcoms, and ball games? Even if I keep my eyes off of impurities, how much time will I want to invest in what doesn't really matter?" [2]

Being tough-minded about godliness means making hard decisions about what we spend our lives doing in the present in light of our future with Christ.

TOUGH-MINDED ABOUT HIS PROMISES (2 PETER 3:12)

Many people think studying the Scriptures concerning the return of the Lord and the inauguration of heaven is a waste of time. But it's not! If that were true, the authors of the New Testament would not have focused on it like they do. Remove all the information about the future from the Bible and you remove about one-fourth of the book. Christ promised that He was going to return to earth, so we need to be tough-minded about that promise and live in light of it.

Peter said that scoffers would come in the last days and mock the promise of Christ's return (2 Peter 3:3–4). But men forget that God doesn't keep time like we do (2 Peter 3:8). All the prophecies in the Old Testament about Christ's first coming were fulfilled, and we can be sure the promises of His Second Coming will be as well.

C. S. Lewis wrote, "I must keep alive in myself the desire for my true country which I shall not find until after my death. I must never let it get snowed under or turned aside. I must make it the main object of life to press on to that other country and help as many as I can, do the very same."[3]

Here are some New Testament exhortations about the return of Christ:

- Philippians 3:20 Wait for Him eagerly.
- Titus 2:13 Watch for His coming.
- Hebrews 9:28 Eagerly wait for His coming.
- 2 Timothy 4:8 Love His appearing.

We need to be tough-minded about Christ's promise to return and not let the world lull us into apathy and ungodliness.

TOUGH-MINDED ABOUT OUR PURPOSE (2 PETER 3:14)

Verse 14 is the third time Peter mentions the idea of being "diligent" (see also 2 Peter 1:5–7, 10). Peter says in verse 14 that, "looking forward to these things" (the coming of Christ and the future renovation of the earth), we are to "be diligent to be found by Him in peace, without spot and blameless." We are to be diligent about our purpose as believers while we await the return of the Lord.

Every believer has been given one or more spiritual gifts—and that certainly should impact our life purpose. We must be diligent in applying those gifts in the body of Christ. It's easy to become a spiritual "couch potato" and lapse into doing nothing—just marking time and taking up space. That is not why God saved us. There are works He saved us to accomplish, and being diligent about our purpose means accomplishing those tasks (Ephesians 2:10). One day we will stand before Christ and give an account of what we have done (or not done) for Him.

I, like you, have opportunities presented to me all the time for how I could invest my time, talent, and treasure. Ninety percent of them I turn down even though they are good things because they don't mesh with God's purpose for my life. We have to be as tough-minded and focused about staying on task in the spiritual life as we do at our daily jobs. Review the apostle Paul's own words to get a good illustration of what it means to stay focused on God's calling (Philippians 3:13–14).

TOUGH-MINDED ABOUT OUR PROFESSION (2 PETER 3:17)

Peter warns his readers about "untaught and unstable people" who try to twist the Scriptures to their own advantage (verse 16). Then he says, since you know they're going to do this, ". . . beware lest you also fall from your own steadfastness, being led away with the error of the wicked."

Not fall from your salvation, but from your steadfastness—from being solidly immovable in your spiritual convictions. When people come to your door peddling a heretical view of Jesus, you are unmoved because you know what you believe. The Bible says that at the end of the age, there is going to be an increase in false teachers and teachings. "Since you know this beforehand," Peter says, "beware." Stand firm in your profession and confession of faith in Jesus.

TOUGH-MINDED ABOUT OUR PROGRESS (2 PETER 3:18)

Finally, we have to be tough-minded about our progress in the faith. The last thing Peter wrote to the Christian church that we have a record of is verse 18: "But grow in the grace and knowledge of our Lord and Savior Jesus Christ. To Him be the glory both now and forever. Amen." There are four ways we make progress in our spiritual growth.

Growth Comes Through the Will of God

Growth is a lifelong process; we never reach the end until we meet Jesus in the air. As much as I have taught the Bible over the last forty years, I still learn new things every time I open it. If you are not different today than you were six months or a year ago, you're not growing.

How do I grow? Physically, we have to eat right, exercise, avoid toxins, and drink clean water. And there are also things we have to do to grow spiritually, not least of which is to abide in the will of God. It is God's will for us to grow spiritually as Paul says in Philippians 1:6: "He who has begun a good work in you will complete it."

Growth Comes Through the Watchfulness of Prayer

Peter writes that ". . . the end of all things is at hand; therefore be serious and watchful in your prayers" (1 Peter 4:7). Prayer may take more tough-mindedness than any other aspect of our spiritual life. Prayer is one of the disciplines of the Christian life that we do out of obedience. Then we find that God meets us there and fills our heart with love and excitement and the desire to pray again. It is a tough-minded choice to get on our knees in the first place, but a choice that leads to growth.

Growth Comes Through the Word of God

Christ said in Revelation 22:7, "Behold, I am coming quickly! Blessed is he who keeps the words of the prophecy of this book." Revelation is the only book that promises a blessing to those who read and keep its words. Jesus said He was coming quickly and that we need to hold on to the words concerning His coming. If you do, you will grow spiritually. If you don't, you will stagnate in your excitement about God's plan for the end of the age.

Growth Comes Through the Work of the Church

Hebrews 10:24–25 says that we are to meet together regularly "in order to stir up love and good works . . . exhorting one another . . . as [we] see the Day approaching." The "Lone Ranger" mentality prevalent among so many Christians today will not result in growth. God designed Christians, like the cells and organs in our body, to grow together. You must be tough-minded about being in church, small groups, and other settings where you can be "stirred up" and "exhorted" by others.

To bring this series to a close, let me quote C. S. Lewis once again. He wrote, "If you have read history, you will find that the Christians who did most for the present world were just those who thought most of the next world. It is since Christians have largely ceased to think of the other world that they have become so ineffective in this world." [4]

My prayer for you, dear friend, is that this series of studies has helped to focus your eyes of faith on that which is yet to come: your heavenly home. And that being more heavenly minded, you will become more earthly good to God and others than you have ever been before.

Notes:

1. Wayne Martindale, *Beyond the Shadowlands: C. S. Lewis on Heaven and Hell* (Wheaton: Crossways, 2005), 46–47.

2. Randy Alcorn, *Heaven* (Wheaton: Tyndale House Publishers, 2004).

3. C. S. Lewis, *Mere Christianity* (New York: Macmillan, 1960) quoted in Randy Alcorn, *Heaven* (Wheaton: Tyndale House Publishers, 2004).

4. C. S. Lewis, *Mere Christianity* (New York: Macmillan, 1960).

1. First Corinthians 15:58 (NIV) has two primary exhortations:

   a. First, stand _____ , let nothing _____ you.

   b. Second, give yourself fully to the_____ of the Lord.

   c. Verse 58 is the conclusion of a long presentation by Paul that takes up all of chapter 15. What did Paul write about in this chapter?

   d. What questions was Paul answering? (verses 12, 35)

   e. So what is the connection between a teaching on death and the resurrection and the exhortations in verse 58? Why would the Corinthians have been tempted to think that their "labor in the Lord [was in] vain"? (verse 58)

   f. Why is the expectation of resurrection and heaven a motivation to continue working hard for the Lord until we die?

   g. What does Paul say in 1 Corinthians 15:14 and 19 that addresses this issue of living in vain?

h. How did Solomon address this issue in Ecclesiastes 1:1-4?

i. How did he ultimately answer his own fears of vanity? (Ecclesiastes 12:13)

j. How does "fear God" serve as a parallel to the New Testament message of "standing firm"? (How does the presence or absence of God in life make the difference between vanity and purposefulness?)

k. What role does the certainty of the resurrection and heaven make in how you live your life?

2. Since the Bible affirms the certainty of the resurrection and eternal life, why is 2 Peter 1:10 a proper exhortation?

a. How certain are you of your own calling and election?

b. What did the apostle John write that allows one to live with certainty about going to heaven? (1 John 5:11-13)

c. What should you do if you are not certain about your calling and election in Christ—not certain about spending eternity in heaven?

The idea of "vanity" is made more clear by the meanings of the original Hebrew and Greek words. In the Old Testament the Hebrew word *hebel* (translated "vain" in Ecclesiastes 1:2) meant vapor or breath—something that had no substance and was easily dissipated. The New Testament Greek word for "vain" is *kenos*—a word that meant empty or empty-handed. In both cases it is easy to see how the English word "vain" was used to translate these original words. A life without certainty of heaven could easily appear to be empty or like a vapor.

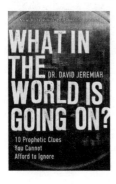

High Definition Giving

High definition has become the ultimate for clarity in television, but what about looking at our stewardship with high definition? This new study guide on stewardship will help the reader learn to focus on not only the purpose in giving, but the joy and blessing we receive as we faithfully give back to God what is His.

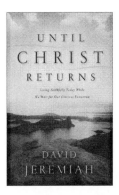

Until Christ Returns

Drawing from the Olivet Discourse in the Book of Matthew, *Until Christ Returns* outlines priorities for believers in an era of heightened stress and confusion. Dr. David Jeremiah reminds us that this is no time for the Church to panic, become distracted, or become confused. Learn more about living in expectation of our Lord's return in *Until Christ Returns*.

Each of these resources was created from a teaching series by Dr. David Jeremiah. Each series is available with correlating study guide and CD audio albums.

For pricing information and ordering, contact us at

P.O. Box 3838
San Diego, CA 92163
(800) 947-1993
WWW.DAVIDJEREMIAH.ORG

STAY CONNECTED
TO DR. DAVID JEREMIAH

Take advantage of two great ways to let Dr. David Jeremiah give you
spiritual direction every day! Both are absolutely FREE

Turning Points Magazine and Devotional

Receive Dr. David Jeremiah's monthly
magazine, *Turning Points* each month:

- Monthly Study Focus
- 48 pages of life-changing reading
- Relevant Articles
- Special Features
- Humor Section
- Family Section
- Daily devotional readings for each
  day of the month
- Bible study resource offers
- Live Event Schedule
- Radio & Television Information

Your Daily Turning Point E-Devotional

Start your day off right! Find words of inspiration
and spiritual motivation waiting for you on your
computer every morning! You can receive a daily
e-devotion communication from David Jeremiah
that will strengthen your walk with God and
encourage you to live the authentic Christian life.

**Sign up for these two free services by visiting us
online at www.DavidJeremiah.org and clicking on
DEVOTIONALS to sign up for your monthly copy
of *Turning Points* and your Daily Turning Point.**